John

It has been a pleasure to meet you & to explore your areas of expertise!

BLOODY COMPUTERS
HOW TO REGAIN CONTROL OF IT SUPPORT COSTS

I look forward to working with you.

Best Wishes

— Sally —

24/3/16

SALLY LATIMER-BOYCE

BLOODY COMPUTERS
HOW TO REGAIN CONTROL OF IT SUPPORT COSTS

Published by
10-10-10 Publishing
1-9225 Leslie St.
Richmond Hill
Ontario, Canada
L4B 3H6

Copyright © September 2015 by Sally Latimer-Boyce
Northamptonshire, England, United Kingdom
www.bloodycomputersbook.com
E: sally@bloodycomputersbook.com I M: +44 (0) 7766 500300

All Rights Reserved
No part of this book may be reproduced in any form, by photocopying or by electronic or mechanical means, including information storage or retrieval systems, without permission in writing from both the copyright owner and the publisher of this book.

For information about special discounts for bulk purchases, please contact 10-10-10 Publishing at 1-888-504-6257

Printed in the United States of America
ISBN - 978-1516943746

Contents

Foreword	v
A Message to the Reader	vii
Dedication	ix
Acknowledgements	xi
Testimonials	xiii
Chapter 1: Prelude	1
Chapter 2: Setting Your Stall	13
Chapter 3: Integrity	23
Chapter 4: People Power	35
Chapter 5: Do it Yourself	45
Chapter 6: Don't Be Hasty	53
Chapter 7: The Unscrupulous	61
Chapter 8: Potential Hazards	69
Chapter 9: Knowledge is Power	81
Chapter 10: Best Practice	93
About the Author	107

Foreword

When I first met Sally I was struck by her professionalism and great ease of communication.

What stands out most about Sally is her passion for her subject, but what makes her unique is her desire to share that knowledge and empower others. Her broad range of IT Support and Consultancy experience places her in the optimum position for writing a book of this nature.

When I read her manuscript it became abundantly clear that she was also able to translate this passion onto paper, which is what makes Bloody Computers so accessible for readers.

This book gives you easy-to-read guidance on the multiple ways to protect your IT budget.

Whether you are a business owner, a network administrator responsible for maintaining multiple PCs or just simply a home user, you will find Bloody Computers a useful resource to change your state of awareness and understanding. With top tips and real life examples, you will have a renewed capacity to effectively protect and defend your IT budget.

This book deserves a place on the shelf of every computer user.

Raymond Aaron
New York Times Best-selling Author

A Message to the Reader

Most people don't really care about computers; they are simply a means to an end – a tool to help you do what you need to do. They can be complex and overwhelming and are known to fail spectacularly, taking all your data with them.

As a computer user, you will know only too well that the cost of owning IT equipment is not limited to the initial purchase. Whether you manage a network of IT systems or own a single device, your equipment will inevitably need support at some stage. System failures, upgrades, application errors and viruses all require third party assistance.

In my chosen career of IT support and consultancy, I have resolved IT issues for thousands of people. I can therefore vouch for the overwhelming costs associated with owning computer equipment. This book shares the things I have learned and will help you break the vicious cycle of support charges.

Bloody Computers is not about making you tech-savvy. It is an insider's guide to eradicating the mystery surrounding technical expertise. This book will empower and enlighten, enabling you to protect your IT budget, and ultimately regain control of IT support costs.

Dedication

I dedicate this book to my amazing, adorable and loving parents Kevin and Ann. For your consistent faith in my abilities and for your continued encouragement of my goals, aspirations and dreams. Thank you for believing in me, and for always being there to listen, guide and support me. Your loving daughter, Sally.

Acknowledgements

I wish to personally thank the following people for their contributions to my inspiration and knowledge. Without your continued faith and support, this book would not have been possible.

James Bedster, the most influential and genuine IT Professional I have met throughout my career. You are a man of great integrity and it is an honor and privilege to work alongside you.

David Boyce, my wonderful husband, for your patience, understanding and unwavered compassion whilst every spare moment of my time was spent writing this book.

Catherine Hickford, for the never-failing support and boundless amounts of encouragement, solidarity and dedication to helping me to get my book done. You are a true inspiration and I owe you so much.

Nigel Higgins, for your frank and forthright approach, and for placing your trust and faith in my abilities. I respect you for your honesty and admire your boundless energy and outstanding achievements.

Mike and Julie Hynd, two of my longest-standing clients, both of whom are incredibly supportive, consistent and kind. I am humbled by your loyalty and working with you is a real pleasure.

David Johnson, for your outstanding professionalism. You are humble, trustworthy and incredibly decent, and your kind nature makes you an absolute pleasure to be around.

Jane Lumley-Walker, for your professionalism, efficiency and incredibly organized approach to everything you do. You never cease to amaze me and it is an absolute pleasure to work with you.

Robert Westgate, for your genuine honesty, loyalty, solidarity and witty banter. Our mutual appreciation for Apple technology unites us, and I will be forever grateful that you introduced me to Craig, Ashley and Karen.

Claire Worley, for your kindness, loyalty and consistently warm welcome. Your boundless energy and attention to detail affords you much respect - you are a breath of fresh air.

Brian Wrigley, the most reliable, consistent, dependable business coach I have ever had the pleasure to work with. Thank you for helping me to achieve my vision and to focus my goals and aspirations.

Testimonials

"As importers and distributors of wiring accessories it is imperative we have efficient up to date IT equipment, software and support. Since our business was founded in 2002 we have been fully supported through our growth by Sally Latimer-Boyce of Serendipiti. Sally's advice is uncomplicated, her delivery of service excellent, and her response to problems or issues is second to none. A truly professional individual who I would thoroughly recommend to any business."
Mike Hynd, SMJ UK Ltd

"In preparation for the opening of additional business premises, we were in need of a new computer system for multiple users. Following an initial consultation with Sally Latimer-Boyce from Serendipiti, our new equipment was delivered and installed by her personally. Everything worked as expected, and she even made numerous follow-up calls to the office to ensure there were no system issues in the days following our opening day. An outstanding service, thank you."
Chris Bailey, Baileys Travel

"A huge thank you Sally, for your expert advice with regards to backup technology and the speed at which you implemented the device remotely. This was just the ticket and the very device I have been looking for. You are a true professional in your field and it is with total pleasure that I would have no hesitation in referring you. A first class service - thank you."
Alan Piggot, Promote-it Ltd

"Yet again Sally, your services for being our 'outsourced insider' have proved invaluable! With one phone call to your office, we received a call back within the hour and via remote support you were able to re-instate our mail flow with minimum fuss. I find your knowledge of our systems amazing. Thank you so much."
Lee Lackford, CVL Systems

"Over the years, Sally Latimer-Boyce from Serendipiti has proved to be an invaluable partner to our company in supporting all of our IT requirements. From the day when our first server based system was installed, she has provided a first class service in terms of software updates, hardware integration and advice. Technical issues are dealt with efficiently to ensure that an IT system which we now rely on so heavily is always functioning. I would have no hesitation in recommending the services of Sally and her company to others business owners."
David Johnson, Meter Mix Systems Ltd

"As a busy PR and marketing company we struggle without IT we can rely on. When our business outgrew the Heath Robinson IT set up that had got us through our first few years, we invited Sally from Serendipiti to install a server and make us professional. And wow, what a difference it has made. Sally completed the installation with the minimum of disruption. Our IT is now totally reliable - everything just works! And on the odd occasion when we do break something, it's great to have expert support just a phone call away. I can focus on running my business knowing that there is someone in the background keeping the IT working."
Paul Green, Growth UK

Chapter 1
Prelude

Preface

I absolutely LOVE technology. Computers, iPads, iPhones; if it is technical, I am all over it!

I carved a career indulging in my passion, and have been providing IT support and consultancy for over three decades. I have handled thousands of support issues, ranging from server installations, to the computers infamous blue screen of death - and everything in between.

Today I am one of two founder-owners of Serendipiti (IT Services) Limited, providing IT consultancy and support services to the business community. I am delighted and incredibly humbled to share a wonderfully loyal client base with my business partner – many of whom have been clients for over 20 years.

Following thirty years service in my chosen field, I am empowered by an in-depth knowledge of how technology impacts the home and business community – especially in relation to the cost of ownership.

Buying a computer or technical device is one thing, but owning it is entirely another. Everything you purchase has a 'cost of ownership' associated to it – in particular third party IT support. Third party IT Support might include:

- Troubleshooting: Assistance to help overcome viruses, application errors, system crashes, data loss – issues which directly impact upon the performance or day-to-day use of your device which is not covered by your manufacturer's warranty.

- Upgrades and repairs: Replacement parts, installations and additional components will need to be managed by an experienced professional.

- Consultancy: Advice regarding upgrades, integration and ongoing development.

- Training: To develop the knowledge of an individual user, or to deploy a corporate policy to ensure a united approach to the use of a specific application.

All of these services cost time and money, and over the lifetime of the device, it is entirely possible for the support costs to exceed the actual purchase price of the equipment. There is a way you can limit the demand for IT support, and ultimately save money.

When it comes to calling upon third party assistance, the advice provided herein will empower you to such an extent that you will seriously slash your IT support costs with immediate effect without compromising the relationship with your provider.

The Early Years

My passion for the 'electronic universe' started as a teenager, when I was introduced to an electronic typewriter at school. I had previously learned to typewrite on a clunky manual device, so I was blown away by the ease of keystrokes afforded by the electronic version. I was both excited and intrigued as to how technology might evolve, and from my first introduction to that marvellous electronic typewriter, I was hooked.

My first experience of a Personal Computer (PC) was equally as memorable. Unlike an electronic typewriter, the PC offered a colour screen, and a graphical user interface. Wow! I didn't realise it at the time, but this was my first encounter of the Microsoft operating system – an introduction that was to change my life forever.

I was working as a secretary when it became apparent I had a natural aptitude for computers. My employer at the time had already recognized that outsourcing IT support was necessary, but he was the first to admit that, whilst he had the vision, he lacked the know-how. So as each new version of Microsoft was released, the organization I worked for hired a local consultant called David to take care of the upgrades.

David was an incredibly patient and knowledgeable consultant, who charged for his services by the hour. My Boss (being particularly savvy and conscious of his ongoing support costs), asked if I would be willing to shadow David to learn what he did, with a view to taking on some of the IT support issues myself. I was ecstatic at the prospect (which is probably more than can be said for poor David).

As David's newly appointed trainee, I asked "why, what, and how" every time he addressed a problem. He would patiently and meticulously explain his methodology. Within three months I was promoted to "Systems Administrator" and soon became the first point of contact for any IT issue. Naturally, I felt a little guilty for directly impacting upon David's income potential, but on reflection I now believe he knew exactly what he was doing.

David clearly embraced the spirit of empowerment by sharing his knowledge, and as his understudy he recognized my desire to learn.

In those early years I lacked confidence and could not help but wonder if it was just luck that was leading me to beat the computer and fix the problem. However, as time passed it was evident that I held a significant understanding of the technology and was soon demonstrating a consistent and proven aptitude for overcoming IT problems. As such, it wasn't long before I was dubbed the "IT expert" by my colleagues.

The positive response to my new-found skill led to a desire to help as many people as possible. My objective to this day is not just to fix the problem, but where possible to empower those that I help.

I wrote this book as a result of my deep-rooted desire to empower others. Whatever your reason for using a computer, the contents will benefit you.

Computerphobia

The 1980s time period brought great social and economic changes, and was undoubtedly the best decade for a teenager to grow up in – ever.

I was the classic 1980s chick (I'd spend countless hours on the dance floor getting my groove on to Spandau Ballet and The Human League), but great music wasn't the only awesome thing to come from that era – we were also blessed with the launch of the Personal Computer. On reflection, I realise that I was the perfect age to embrace technology – being introduced to it from the start I was essentially able to grow up with it. But unbeknownst to me at the time, I was in the minority - it turns out that technology was not necessarily as well received as I had imagined.

According to Technology Researchers Gartner Inc, there were one billion computers in use by 2008. It is now estimated to be closer to two billion. Computers rapidly permeated our homes and offices – and with them came a new form of consumer anxiety – 'Computerphobia'.

I recall realising very quickly that computers were not as intriguing and desirable to the masses as I naively first thought. Even some of my own school friends displayed the classic symptoms of Computerphobia - which were listed by Gartner to include:
1. a reluctance to physically touch the device for fear of damaging it
2. a fear of looking stupid
3. feeling threatened by 'computer alphas' who know all about them

Often, sufferers would resign themselves to a life of just managing computer symptoms, accepting that they might never understand them.

In my experience, computerphobic people fall into one of two categories; those who believe computers are really clever and those who believe computers are stupid. The truth is, a computer is neither. It is simply a machine that can only do as it is told. It is not possible for it to be either intelligent or stupid. A computer is restricted to a finite amount of predetermined code and is unable to apply judgement or experience to resolving problems. With guidance even the most self-confessed technophobe with extreme 'Computerphobia' can get to grips with the basics and embrace it with more confidence.

Learning to use a computer is less like following written instructions and more like taking up a musical instrument. It takes time, practice and patience.

I linked my affinity to computers with my musical background. Music helped me to develop my concentration. Furthermore, it taught me perseverance and enhanced my co-ordination and maths skills – all of which became prerequisites for a career as an IT professional.

There is a cure for Computerphobia! It is possible to abandon this fear. Like learning an instrument, it will take a little practice but in time you too can enjoy the harmony a little perseverance and determination can bring.

> "The human spirit must prevail over technology"
> – Albert Einstein.

Technology is nothing to be afraid of - it is merely a skill set. Embrace it, and you too will be empowered.

Computer says No

As consumers, we encounter technology on a day-to-day basis. Almost without exception, the person serving us at the store or petrol station is doing so with the help of an electronic device. The objective of the equipment is far and wide – but essentially it is designed to enhance the consumer experience and improve the productivity of the company providing the service.

Delighting customers these days is no longer dependent solely upon the personality and spirit of the employee assigned to serving you.

But just how much onus should we place on the equipment, and can we really afford to design out all traces of human intervention in the name of productivity?

I recently reserved a hotel room. At the point of booking, I asked for breakfast and dinner to be included. After I had checked in, I visited the restaurant. After referring to the screen of her ordering system, the waitress informed me that the meal package I had paid for included a choice of wine or beer.

I rarely drink alcohol, so I asked if I could have a soft drink instead. After several taps on her screen the waitress declined my request on account that "the computer won't let me do that." I presumed she would then add "but let me see what I can do" but alas no. To my astonishment this was her final thought on the subject, because the computer had essentially said no.

Whilst the computer system she was using did not afford her the flexibility needed to change the transaction on screen, it was not unreasonable of me as the customer to request that she overrule it.

The introduction of IT equipment was never intended to replace the art of decision-making. Of course reducing the need for employees to make decisions in a process-driven environment can be very effective, but (as this example demonstrates) if this is taken to the extreme it can also be incredibly unproductive.

Further time was wasted when the waitress elected to call upon a manager to make the decision. Eventually, they reluctantly agreed to provide me with a soft drink. Not quite my idea of an quality service.

Embracing technology does not mean one should abandon the responsibility to communicate as a human being.

When assigned charge of a computer, in any environment, remember that the computer is not able to make decisions. Unlike humans, computers cannot use judgement or experience to figure out a solution. Avoid falling into the trap of allowing the computer the final say.

A Man's World

My husband David is a Computer Aided Design Engineer. Our son James, who is now 14, has always marveled that his Dad gets paid to draw all day.

James has grown up with the knowledge that both of his parents understand computers. Although my husband shares my love of Information Technology, his particular field is rather specialist. He would therefore be the first to agree that his line of work does not lend itself to keeping abreast of all the typical IT issues that many users experience on a day-to-day basis.

Consequently, when issues arose on our home computer, it was inevitable that I would be the one to fix the problem.

One Sunday afternoon when James was only five years old, something intriguing happened at home. James and I had been playing on the computer when, without warning, the computer crashed and the blue screen of death appeared.

James immediately turned to Dave and said "Daddy can you fix the computer?" He was too young to recall that I had always fixed such problems in our home – instead he has simply assumed it was a man's job.

This was a pivotal point in my career. I had already set up a successful IT Support company by this point, and it had not once occurred to me that I was operating in a male-dominated industry. I had a genuine heartfelt passion for my chosen field. Combined with my previous experience of IT support I was able to demonstrate my credibility.

So why are there so few female IT consultants? Lifestyle may be one aspect. Unpredictable income and long hours can interfere with family ties. Another reason may be saturation - women might actively participate, but their participation is drowned out by the guys. The more contentious the issue, the less the women are heard.

Whatever the reason, I have always believed in equality and I believe the right person should get the job. As a woman in a predominantly male-orientated industry, I can say with absolute integrity that I make a valid contribution to my field. I am not better, or worse – just different. I can bring a different perspective and set of strengths to the table. Whether those variations come from nature or nurture is irrelevant.

Being in the minority does not undermine my value. I discovered my passion and ran with it, and I have never let the statistics define me.

Embrace your skills and show the world what you are capable of.

Jargon

Technical jargon refers to words or expressions that are difficult for others to understand without specialist knowledge. The problem with jargon is that, unless we understand what we are being told, we cannot make an informed decision.

When we come across this in the world of IT, being on the receiving end of jargon can trigger all sorts of reactions from the technophobe or even result in a full blown case of Computerphobia!

Technical jargon is not just limited to the spoken word. Instruction booklets and end-user guides can carry so much complicated wording that in reality only another engineer could hope to make sense of them.

There is often an assumed level of knowledge expected in the recipient, which is not necessarily present. When I became a reseller of software packages, I would usually insist that the software provider supplies a user manual. Sadly the 'End-User-Guides' they subsequently provided were excessively unwieldy – and not suited to the client whose priority was to be up and running quickly.

The guides were more like system administrator guides – written by an expert, for an expert. No one wants to wade through a 60 page PDF to resolve a simple 'how-to', so I found myself writing end user guides to fill the void of literature tailored to the individual end user.

Whether it is a car mechanic or IT professional - the onus is on them to deliver the information without jargon. They have a duty of care to reiterate without patronizing, and reputable professionals will take time to ensure their communications have been received and understood.

As consumers we have a responsibility too. If you do not understand what has been explained, ask for it to be explained again. If you are exchanging payment for a service, it is crucial for you to make an informed decision.

Don't be afraid to ask for instructions to be provided in plain English.

It is YOUR system – be sure to understand what is being explained. If you don't understand first time, don't be afraid to say so. No reputable professional will object to going over instructions again - they want you to understand and make the most from your investment.

Chapter 2
Setting Your Stall

Be Proactive

The most effective way to keeping a lid on your IT costs is to find an IT support company or professional you can trust, and stick with them. Having a history with one support provider will not only enhance productivity, it will facilitate familiarity with your setup and will help keep your costs low. But how do you differentiate between the best of the bunch, and the undesirables?

Whether you are looking for a new IT support provider because you have never had one before, or you are looking to change providers due to being unhappy with the service you are getting from your current supplier, the prerequisite to finding a trustworthy and reliable support contact is to be proactive.

In other words – avoid making a distressed purchase. Find someone before your next IT issue occurs.

Waiting until after you have suffered a computer problem may lead to you being overly spontaneous, and could have disastrous consequences on both your time and your pocket.

I admit, I don't ever recall waking up on a Sunday morning, putting on my slippers, pouring a coffee, and suddenly thinking to myself "I really must find a plumber just in case we spring a leak in the bathroom." But if you need third-party support of any kind, finding a supplier proactively and BEFORE the next issue occurs is key to ensuring that you find the right support in advance of that next emergency.

How do you go about finding a suitable IT support company?

Before we focus on the do's, let's look at the do not's:

Do not rely on the internet or local directory. Reaching out to a stranger exposes your infrastructure to huge risks, since you will have no way to verify their claim to be trustworthy or reliable.

Do not approach the guy down at the pub. Seeking IT support from the guy down at the pub is asking for trouble. Unless you are 100% sure he is geared up to offering the kind of services you need, leave the chap alone to enjoy his beer in peace.

Do not ask a friend. Mates-rates can be very appealing, but unless he is operating a bonafide IT consultancy, and you are paying the going rate for his services, you can rest assured that a friend is unlikely to offer you priority support.

Fortunately, finding the right IT consultant is far easier than you think. But there are some very important things you must do before you make that call - you must first define your vision.

Define your Vision

Before you consider appointing a third party IT support provider, it is crucial that you have a road map of your IT requirements including what you have now, and what your vision is for your setup in the future.

You do not need any technical know-how to define your vision. Just be as open and indulgent with your vision as possible – once you have found the right IT support company to help you, they will have an abundance of experience to help you deploy that vision. The important thing at this stage is to get your vision down in writing.

There are two parts to your vision:
1. what you have now
2. What you want for the future

Document your current setup: For example, you may be a business owner, and have five computers (of varying ages) which are already networked together for file sharing. Your existing setup works for you, but it is a little slow and you know your systems can do more. You may also recognize that you need to replace some equipment.

Documenting what you have now is beneficial on so many levels. Not only does it provide you with a snapshot of your IT setup, it will also provide you with an accurate inventory of your systems. This can be put to further use for the safe keeping of other critical information such as make, model and age of the computer, not to mention usernames and passwords.

I personally refer to such documentation as the "IT Fingerprint". An IT Fingerprint will be hugely beneficial to your appointed IT consultant and is likely to save you money when they arrive to carry out an information gathering exercise.

Your vision for the future: In order to establish a vision for the future, you simply need to ask yourself, what are all the things you aspire to? If users require training, add this to your vision; if the computers are slow, add improved performance to your vision. Getting some clarify on what you want will provide you with some scope for discussions with your support company, and will ensure that you are invested in any recommended solutions. Knowledge is power, and if you have a rough vision to press forward with you will feel more confident when discussions begin with your consultant. Additionally, you will have more buying power.

Your vision may be grand and indulgent – or it may be very simple. Whatever form it takes, it is important for you to know it before you commence your search for a suitable IT support provider.

Once you have a draft IT Fingerprint, and have documented your vision, you are now ready to look for a support provider that is a good fit.

For a sample IT Fingerprint,
visit www.bloodycomputersbook.com/samples

Recommendations

For over fifteen years, I have been a member of a networking organization known as The Business Network International (BNI). It is a referrals organization where I go to promote my own company.

As a member of BNI, I meet with members of other local companies every week. This provides the opportunity to regularly promote my IT support services by way of a weekly 60-second presentation. To keep it interesting and varied, I deliver a different topic every time, and in doing so I build knowledge and confidence in my fellow members. Members call upon my services, and recommend me to their own contacts. The reason BNI is so beneficial to me is because it works on the principle of recommendation.

Being a member of BNI has enabled me to build relationships and trust in my fellow members - which means I can recommend their services too. If I call upon a member whose services I have never used before, I can simply ask another member to vouch for the quality of the service they provide.

You do not need to be a member of BNI to source an IT consultant through recommendation. You just need a recommendation from someone you trust. A vast majority of my clients came through recommendations from other clients.

Once you have your vision, you will be able to ask someone you know (a supplier, client or other contact) who has already achieved some or all of your vision with their own IT setup of a similar scale and size, and ask them who they can recommend. Approach more than one contact too, and you may even find the same IT consultant is recommended to you multiple times.

Stick with local contacts first, because they are more likely to utilize a local IT support provider. That said, it should not be considered a deal breaker if you find you are recommended to a company outside of your region – just be sure to ask about travel costs as you do not want to incur charges for a consultant's two hour journey to get to you.

You would do well to ask many questions when gathering information about your prospective provider – How efficient are they? How many phases did the project take to complete? And where possible ask about support costs.

Provided your contacts can vouch for the quality of service provided, you will not only save yourself time and hassle, you will stand a better chance of appointing a professional you can trust - from the start.

Recommendations are the safest, most cost-effective way to secure third-party IT support. Take time to make the right decision and don't rush into a relationship with the wrong company.

> For more information about the BNI,
> go to www.bloodycomputersbook.com/bni

Face to Face

You have scoped out your requirements and obtained a list of recommended support providers from someone you know and trust, and who has a similar setup to the one defined in your vision.

Now you are now ready to meet face to face with the company or consultant who has been highly recommended.

It is important that you meet face to face to discuss your requirements, and the agenda for that first meeting should be driven by you. This is your opportunity to discuss your vision for the future, as well as understand some of the finer points of your proposed new relationship. You need to feel comfortable with the responses they provide when you share your vision and goals.

The key focal points of your agenda for the meeting should be:
- Vision - your chance to share your vision
- Charges - how will you be charged for their support services
- Contracts - are you expected to sign a contract, and do these contracts provide value for money?
- Continuity - can they assure you a commitment to continuity?
- Integrity - do they lead by example?

These topics are covered in detail within the next few chapters. When arranging the meeting, ask who will be attending. If the meeting is being handled by a sales representative, he or she is more likely to be scripted and less likely to genuinely and accurately assure you of their ability to meet your needs. Ask if you can meet with the IT consultant directly - ie. the person who will be looking after your site. This will give you the opportunity to get a gut feel about whether or not you are a good fit, and allow you to determine the nature of the person you will be working with. It is important that you gel with this person too, since they will be looking after your staff. The last thing you want is to feel dismissed or patronized. People buy people, so be sure to take on the right person for you and your team from the start.

You would not ordinarily expect to pay for an initial meeting of this kind. However, it is important that you avoid asking the consultant to address any IT issues on the day of the visit. Get the paperwork out of the way first - discuss and agree to the terms of your alliance before you ask him to get into any technical fixes. The consultant can always be scheduled to return, once you have established what it will cost you.

Only after the first meeting has concluded, and all agreements been made in writing, should you consider moving to the next step of your relationship - the site survey.

Site Survey

A site survey brings mutual benefit to both parties. If you have a site of more than 2 or 3 computers, a site survey is likely to be recommended by your newly-appointed IT consultant. However, if you have fewer than two computers, you might find the consultant performs a very basic review of the systems, and this will probably be performed remotely.

A detailed site survey should only be agreed to after you have appointed the consultant. A lot of crucial and confidential information is captured during a review of your site, so unless you are happy to share this information, do not permit a review until you have agreed the terms of your alliance.

From your perspective, a site survey will enable your new support representative to capture information regarding your setup that can subsequently be added to your existing inventory. It will also open some dialogue in relation to the vision you previously shared at your first meeting, and should help to ensure that everyone is on the same page.

From the consultant's perspective, performing a detailed site survey will enable him or her to familiarize themself with the existing setup, taking in all relevant information that you may have overlooked during your initial meeting.

In order to achieve a detailed survey, he or she will need to spend 5-10 minutes looking at each computer, noting the operating system, make/model, and any issues the end user might have.

Additional devices would be examined too, such as servers, printers and other network equipment.

Once again, the most appropriate person to perform the site survey is the person who will predominately be looking after your account.

Following the survey, you should expect to receive written communication which clearly outlines the information the supplier has captured on your behalf (ie. A formal copy of the IT Fingerprint). It is important that the consultant commits to maintaining this document (with you, or on your behalf), so that with each visit or IT fix, the document can be updated, allowing it to evolve into a comprehensive inventory of crucial system-related information.

Following the survey, the consultant should be in a position to provide you with any recommendations that are necessary to help you achieve your vision. You should also then be able to start calling upon IT support at your leisure - both reactively and proactively.

Continuity

When it comes to IT support, continuity is hugely important - not just for the sake of efficiency, but as a way of keeping IT support costs down.

If you have ever been admitted to hospital, you will be familiar with the issue surrounding continuity. As a patient you are likely to have encountered a variety of specialists who, for one reason or another, have had a brief amount of time to become acquainted with your case history. The opportunity for you to build a rapport with the specialist is diminished, which could leave you lacking confidence in the proposed treatment.

A new client approached me recently, citing a frustration with the lack of continuity provided by their existing support personnel. Every time the client had a problem, they were sent a different engineer, not because he happened to be more experienced in dealing with that particular issue, but because he was the first one available.

This caused all sorts of problems because the visiting engineer would need to spend an inordinate amount of time getting to know the setup, and often asking the client for information that in truth should have already been known to him. They also confirmed that, in some cases, the second engineer would undo the work of the first, but the client would still be charged for it.

Your site is unique, and it will have a history of various nuances that can be more effectively supported by someone who knows your setup inside out. In order to provide you with a decent level of continuity, ask your IT support company to assign a key account manager who is technically able to take care of your entire IT setup.

Of course expecting an account manager to be available 24/7 is neither practical nor sustainable, because they will be entitled to annual leave. Therefore, in addition to a dedicated account manager it is crucial that the support contact has a system that ensures crucial information is stored safely on your behalf (ie. the "IT Fingerprint").

A document of this kind will ensure that in the absence of your account manager, his colleague will be able to support your site seamlessly, without first having to familiarize himself with the setup.

Without this documentation you may be exposed to a lack of continuity, through no fault of your own, and worse still you may incur additional support charges whilst they bring themselves up to speed at your expense.

When someone understands your IT history, a more effective outcome can be achieved.

Chapter 3
Integrity

Lead by Example

Unsolicited telephone sales calls - we have all picked up the phone to a complete stranger, who has the audacity to ask "How are you today?" before launching into an unwelcome speech about how his miracle product will wow you. Whilst he rambles on about the discounts you can enjoy if you buy in the next 5 minutes, you are busy plotting a creative way to get him off the phone.

If you already have an appointed IT support advisor, you would be wise to get a second opinion before making any rush decisions on anything presented to you by a stranger that, regardless, might have grabbed your attention. But what if your tech support guy is the one promoting this new product to you?

How can you tell the difference between having the software you want, and having what he wants you to have?

I am not referring to version upgrades of existing software products, or even solutions that were discussed as part of your long-term vision. I am referring to those recommendations that might be made entirely out of the blue and are not in the least bit topical to anything you have discussed in the past.

You trust him, of course, so why might you need to be guarded about what he is offering?

The very nature of the industry means that IT support types will have many hundreds of customers. This makes IT support companies a perfect target for the software manufacturers to sell to - enticing them to become resellers in exchange for extremely generous margins. Sadly, some might find the deals just too good to miss and, before long, your tech support guy might find himself signing up as a reseller and subsequently recommending products to his clients for all the wrong reasons.

Worse still, the software providers do not impose strict regulations on their resellers to attend lengthy training courses to learn the appropriate installation techniques. Instead, most leave the resellers to their own devices, which can only spell trouble for the client.

So how can you safeguard against this? First, ask the consultant recommending the product if they are using this product in-house. If it is such a great product, it would be entirely reasonable to expect them to be using it in-house. If they are not using the product, ask what training and experience they have had in installing and supporting the product. If they value your relationship they will be entirely transparent and, where applicable, will advise you upfront if their knowledge of the product is limited.

Provided they can give you a damned good reason why you need to invest in this solution, you may decide to proceed anyway, but at least you will be moving forward on the basis of transparency - aware of the fact that for this particular product you may be learning together.

If in any doubt, defer the recommendation for a few months to allow yourself time to review and consider the benefits in your own time, and the consultant more time to gain experience of the product.

If the solution is really that good, it will still be available at a later date.

Billing Practices

Sadly I have encountered many business owners who, unwittingly, have found themselves caught out by unexpected hidden charges in relation to IT support.

Every support provider levies their fees in a unique way, so identifying and flushing out those hidden costs before you commence your alliance is the best way to safeguard your IT support budget.

Giving and receiving IT support is not just a simple case of raising a support ticket, and waiting for the job to be fixed. There are many other governing factors that can throw a support incident into billing ambiguity:

Travel: unexpected travel costs might be levied if an engineer has to be deployed to site.

Priority response: A premium rate could be imposed if emergency support is needed.

Out of hours: Support given out of hours may be charged at a higher rate.

Imagine that you have raised a support enquiry that is not particularly urgent. Your tech guy takes 24 hours to get to it, but spends less than one minute fixing it. How much would you expect to be charged?

What if that same enquiry had been urgent? Would you be happy to pay a premium for the privilege of securing priority response - even if the task only took 1 minute to fix?

What if you have issues that need to be managed outside of office hours? Would you be surprised to be charged time and a half or double time?

Understanding the billing process before taking them on will eliminate any unexpected surprises, and will ensure your alliance is based on a foundation of trust. If you do not ask the question in advance, you may be setting yourself up for micro-billing. I have inherited many clients who had previously fallen victim to the greedy technician who charged a full hour for just one minute of work – even though the job wasn't urgent.

Ensure your outsourced IT provides a rapid response for critical events and ask what impact priority responses will have on cost.

In my humble opinion, priority response and one-minute fixes should be forthcoming within the spirit of goodwill. This is a perfect opportunity for the supplier to demonstrate their loyalty and commitment, rather than to gain undue benefit from their client's time-sensitive predicament.

Use it or lose it

When it comes to spending money, you expect to receive something of equal value in return. A fair exchange facilitates peace of mind.

Paying for motor insurance does not feel like a fair exchange. We pay it because we are required to do so by law, so we reluctantly accept that we will not see a return on our investment. Often we choose to pay monthly, to make the ongoing cost more palatable.

But unless we are paying out of legal obligation, or to protect ourselves from the loss of something valuable, why would we pay for anything on a regular basis unless we were getting a true return?

When it comes to IT support, unless you are happy to give your hard-earned cash away, the payment scheme to avoid at all costs is the 'use it or lose it' package. Of course, it is never actually called this - but by any other name, this arrangement will cost you money (often on a monthly basis) with little or no return.

An example of this is the 'unlimited support' scheme, where you pay a fixed amount per month whether you call upon support or not.

My concern is this. If payment has been made, and support not received to the equivalent value in return, why should you lose the value of your original investment? Would it not be more advantageous if any unused service is deferred to when you need it most?

These schemes are far from cost-effective, because during busy times you will be less focused on IT issues and more focused on your day-to-day business requirements. Several months can go by before you realize you have forgotten to utilize the service you have been paying for. The point is you shouldn't have to conjure up IT issues just to maximize the return on your investment.

The bottom line is, schemes like this are not designed to benefit you. Support is like any other product; once paid for, it should be delivered upon. If you want to defer 'delivery' of that product, as a paying client you should be entitled to do so - schemes that serve only one party should be avoided at all costs.

Hardware maintenance agreements also characterize these disastrous schemes, where companies were encouraged to pay a monthly fee for an equipment replacement service in the event of failure. There was more justification in the days when computer components were unreliable, difficult to source and expensive to replace. But these days' computer components are cheap and reliable, and as such, these agreements deserve to be laid to rest along with Microsoft Windows 95 and all those other legacy solutions nobody wants anymore.

Beware the awful 'Retainer Schemes' too. These essentially charge for the privilege of having an IT professional on 'standby'. This is both shallow and pretentious and in this highly competitive market, it is entirely unnecessary to pay to retain the services of anyone - no matter how incredible they claim to be.

Check that the support company you are considering offers a support plan that operates within the parameters of fair trading, and leave those who want money for nothing to their own shallow devices.

Twelve-Month Commitment

Commitment. Some of us struggle with it, others sign on the dotted line without a thought. But when it comes to IT support, is it really reasonable to be asked to commit to 12 months?

To the unwitting, agreeing to a twelve-month support contract with your IT representative might seem like no big deal. You anticipate the service will be great and that you will have no reason to back out of the arrangement.

But ask yourself this. Why exactly are you being forced to commit to twelve months?

Is it really necessary to pledge your commitment in writing, thus promising to use their IT support services for a given duration? Surely if this particular company provides an excellent, outstanding service, you will want to keep using them anyway, so who exactly is the twelve-month contract protecting - you or them?

Relationships are at the forefront of any IT support arrangement. Trust and confidence builds up over time, so what happens if, for one reason or another, you stop seeing eye to eye?

Additionally, what if your circumstances change and you no longer want or need the service being offered?

If either of these events occurs within the first month of a twelve-month contract, chances are you will be able to execute an escape clause in your contract. But if it happens three months in, you might be able to part company but you may still be liable for a further nine months worth of payments on the item or service you committed to.

If your arrangement is not built on goodwill, trust and quality of service, both sides can become complacent. The true spirit of good IT support is to be invited to utilize their services because you want to, not because you are contractually obliged to do so.

My wonderful clients are testimony to how loyal people can be without a contract – and I really wouldn't have it any other way.

Stick with reputable companies who offer a degree of transparency and who are willing to demonstrate their worth without forcing you to commit your allegiance for a whole twelve months.

The Limited Unlimited

The idea of paying a fixed price for something unlimited is extremely enticing. We all love the thought of 'all you can eat ice-cream' and those splendid 'open buffets', but just how unlimited is it really?

If food is the offering, there is a limit – not in produce, but in consumption. There is only so much we can eat in one sitting and unless invited to stay the whole day, the so-called unlimited offer is in truth limited to what you can eat in a given time constraint.

IT support is something that is available on an unlimited basis too - though only from a select few. For you the client, there are some perceived benefits to unlimited support – notwithstanding the fact that, no matter what goes wrong with your computer, you need not worry about how long a consultant spends fixing your problem because you are covered by your unlimited support arrangement. Or are you?

Some of the unlimited arrangements I have come across are far from unlimited. The support company takes a fixed amount of money from their client in exchange for an unlimited amount of IT support, but there is so much more to it than just that simple trade.

To provide this service, the support company will need a high volume of technical staff to be able to meet the demands of their client base. With so many different engineers assigned to your account, you can waive goodbye to any shred of continuity.

Even if you are lucky enough to be assigned the same engineer, chances are the objective for them is to protect their costs by attending only to the problem you have reported. If that engineer has a busy day, chances are your other IT issues may just have to wait.

Of course, not all support companies offering this service are focused on their own costs. If you are fortunate enough to find an arrangement of this kind where the engineer is happy to indulge you and any ad-hoc issues you may have, then great – hold onto them and never let them go. But the reality is that, no matter how honorable the intentions, there is one factor that creeps in and quickly destroys the spirit of the arrangement for both parties – human nature.

From the perspective of the consultant, it will be in his interest to spend as little time on site as possible, in order to maximize the yield gained from your monthly payments. To achieve this, he may want to get the job done quickly. He is less likely to check other areas of a system, or make pro-active recommendations that could make a difference to your productivity or infrastructure.

From your perspective as the client, 'unlimited' undeniably invokes the human instinct to indulge. With unlimited support at your disposal, the desire to find IT issues that need to be fixed can be overwhelming – especially if several months have passed without you needing to call support.

The bottom line is, this arrangement might sound wonderful, but in reality it is neither constructive nor efficient. In practice, it is just another "use it or lose it scheme."

Any arrangement that requires you to take the risk with your hard-earned cash should be avoided at all costs. Find a solution that allows you to budget your IT spend, without any loss of revenue.

Goodwill

The absence of goodwill is common these days, especially in the world of IT. I hear many stories about the breakdown of a relationship between a customer and their IT support provider, but they usually amount to the same thing – an absence of mutual goodwill.

I learnt the value of giving and receiving goodwill early in my career. There is no doubt in my mind as to the importance of delivering client satisfaction and loyalty, and creating a goodwill bank account. It is vital to both parties in a service-based environment. The more goodwill within the business relationship, the greater the impact of overall motivation for all concerned.

Building rapport, operating with integrity and making it easy to work together are all great ways to build goodwill.

Even a relationship between a client and a support provider is non-sustainable if the goodwill is being extended from one side only. If one party is frequently going that extra mile, delivering above and beyond in the name of goodwill - but consistently receiving grief, contempt and unreasonable demands in exchange, the relationship will suffer in the long term. And this applies to both sides.

I have had to recover clients from the clutches of their previous IT support many times, and the sad fact is, if there is an imbalance of goodwill, the support provider is just as likely to walk away from the client as the client is from the provider.

An example of a goodwill imbalance was demonstrated by a new client who indicated that his IT support was refusing to release the administrator password for his server. This client informed me that the password was being withheld because his support representative was just poor at providing a service.

It later materialized that the password had been withheld due to consistent non-payment from the client - which resulted in a severe breakdown of the relationship, and the subsequent withdrawal of goodwill by the support company.

Interestingly, during my endeavors to help, I found the consultant to be genuinely helpful, and the client to be rude and belligerent - even to me. His obvious unwillingness to build goodwill cost him dearly - not only did he part company with his previous IT guy, I also declined to take him on as a client.

Building goodwill is a two-way exchange. It is about doing what is right, being respectful and courteous, and treating others as you would like to be treated.

Build goodwill with your IT consultant and you will both reap the rewards of a long and mutually prosperous alliance.

Chapter 4
People Power

Unconsciously Competent

When it comes to resolving IT issues, many end users will automatically reach out to IT support. Whilst this is entirely understandable, there are occasions when this may lead to a missed opportunity of self-help and reduced support costs.

The fact is, many users are actually very skilled and knowledgeable - they just don't know it. I call this 'unconsciously competent'.

Some end users are quite adept at grasping specific steps and processes (whether they have been shown by tech support or figured it out for themselves) and yet they resist the temptation to come to the aid of a colleague, even though they have a pretty good idea how to fix the problem.

Why are end users not sharing their skill sets with their colleagues, and helping one another fix their own IT problems?

Notwithstanding the fact they may not be authorized to do so, they are likely to be afraid of breaking something. They may have tried to help in the past, only to be shot down by a co-worker, or they might lack confidence and be afraid of getting it wrong.

If users were confident enough to share what they know, and their knowledge harvested and shared with other employees, the truth is that dependency upon IT support would reduce massively.

Specifically, basic tasks that tech support may have just talked a competent end user through could be put to good use if that individual were to be empowered to share their knowledge with others.

Let me give you an example: A computer user calls tech support. The fix was a few clicks away and the end user understood the instruction. Five minutes later, a colleague two desks away from the first employee phones tech support with the same issue. Of course tech support will help, but it might have been just as easily handled by that first member of staff (given half a chance).

Multiply this by 15-20 end users, and you have yourself a whole two hours of IT support charges that could have been handled in-house. At the very least, consider implementing a method for staff to share troubleshooting tips with one another.

Alternatively, if you recognize an end user with a natural ability and flair for grasping IT, consider assigning them as the first point of contact for all IT issues. Even the responsibility of collating IT enquiries in the first instance is a good start, since it will eliminate duplication. With the right training, that appointed individual may even be able to resolve the issue directly.

With the right guidance from tech support, it is entirely possible to empower one end user to act as front line support - reducing the dependency on external support.

Shadow your Consultant

The idea of Shadowing an IT consultant may seem like a crazy idea. If he or she is engaged in IT fixes that you do not feel adequately equipped to understand, why would there be any benefit to shadowing them?

If you have been fortunate enough to identify an individual member of staff who has demonstrated an interest and aptitude in IT, enabling that member of staff to shadow the consultant will be worth its weight in gold.

Nominating a member of staff to act as the initial point of contact for IT support enquiries will not only streamline the entire process for requesting IT support, it will enhance it too. Duplicate issues can be filtered out, and with the right training that individual can be empowered to field some of the enquiries in-house.

I have spent my entire career empowering others in this way - and as a full time IT support consultant I applaud everyone who has assigned a member of staff to shadow me.

There are literally hundreds of tasks that an appointed member of staff can be trained to undertake, and with a degree of patience and goodwill, the saving the client can expect to make from an arrangement of this kind is huge.

Dependent upon the level of security you are prepared to extend, this individual could be empowered to take care of system-related issues across the entire spectrum of your IT equipment; from restarting your server, to checking workstations' and laptops' anti-virus software or windows updates, as well as configuring new users and resetting passwords. Obviously you would need to agree an appropriate security level for this individual, and defer anything outside of that level to your external technical support.

There are no skill prerequisites needed on the part of the selected individual either. As long as they are enthusiastic and have an aptitude and flair for IT, this is often enough to nurture and develop their skills.

Of course, in order for this to work correctly, it would be prudent to announce the new responsibilities of this person to other staff members. Unless the individual is officially recognized as the collator of IT Support enquiries, you may find other members of staff will bypass him or her and continue to report issues direct to external support.

If managed efficiently, the value of this alliance to the individual employee is immense too. The training they will be afforded from tech support will evolve their skills and will provide a wonderful sense of self-worth and value. Incidentally, a suitable title for this role is "Systems Administrator" (this was the title afforded me when I first started out shadowing tech support).

Don't be afraid to appoint a member of staff to adopt the role. Once you see what this will save you in IT support costs, you will be truly glad you did.

I Forgot to Mention

There are several inevitable things that occur when an IT consultant is called to site to address IT support issues, which relate specifically to your staff. If left unmanaged, the consequences to the productivity of that consultant can have costly consequences, so be sure you are familiar with the issues before unleashing your IT professional on your team.

Bloody Computers

To give you an example, your IT support consultant has arrived to assist with some issues that you have. The person responsible for consolidating the support enquiries had already provided him with a list of issues and agreed to the duration and costs in relation to the consultant's time.

The consultant is ready to attend to the first computer or device on the list. As the consultant navigates his way through the task list, it is necessary for him to engage with your staff. This is where some new problems can begin.

All too frequently, staff members forget to report their IT issues. Understandably, they may have been too busy to mention it so have just been putting up with the issue. At other times it might be a genuine case that they feel embarrassed to bring it up. Either way, the sight of the familiar face of IT support is the trigger for additional IT support issues coming out of the woodwork.

At this point, the desire to offload the IT issues to the tech guy is overwhelming. Of course the support representative will want to be accommodating, and out of courtesy is likely to engage that member of staff. However, the downside is that this may add a significant amount of time to his visit. Not only will this result in a possible overspend in IT support, the order of priority may also be compromised.

The best way to avoid this is to instruct your employees to refer their issues to your systems administrator, before the support consultant arrives. Better still, create a form that will enable the employees to quickly and easily report their IT issues the moment they occur.

Also, letting your employees know that a consultant is scheduled to attend on a specific day will ensure they are willing to vacate their computer so the issues can be addressed.

The most effective way to keep a lid on IT costs is for everyone to be in the loop about what needs doing. The consultant can remain focused, you are more aware, and the employee is reassured that his previously reported issues are scheduled to be resolved.

> For a sample support enquiry form, visit
> www.bloodycomputersbook.com/samples

Not now

Your supervisor has committed you to a deadline, which requires you to hammer out a report on your computer. You've barely had time to have a sip of coffee, let alone a lunchbreak. Mid-morning, out of the corner of your eye you catch a glimpse of the one person who can turn your already stretched day into your worst nightmare – IT support! You just know he is going to ask you to vacate your seat so he can fix the problem you reported a few days ago, but why does it have to be now?

This is an all too familiar scene, caused by a breakdown in communication between the person appointing the IT professional, and the end user whose computer has the problem.

Of course, the consultant will be sympathetic - it is a familiar hazard when asking an employee to surrender their desk at a moment's notice, but it can be an awkward moment too. Both the appointed consultant and the end user have a level of authority afforded to them to access the computer, but if the end user decides that now really is not a good time, other than to mildly protest and reschedule with that employee, there really is little the consultant can do but to move on to the next computer.

Bloody Computers

The challenge is that all too often this event has been observed by other members of staff and suddenly the unwillingness of an employee to vacate their seat can become contagious. The colleague who has been listening from the next desk might also claim to be too busy and ask if the consultant can come back later.

I am not trying to suggest that an IT support representative is the most important person in this scenario, and must therefore be given priority. I am simply trying to demonstrate that, from time to time, the consultant's list of tasks may not be deployed as smoothly as one might hope.

Of course if the consultant has multiple IT issues to attend to, he or she can just move on to the next task and return to the unavailable PC later. But if this is the only computer needing attention, delays will just add unnecessary time (and possible charge) to the visit.

Bear in mind also that the employee is unlikely to be aware that the consultant is on the clock unless he or she is the bill payer, so will have a different perspective on the situation.

To overcome these challenges, introduce a simple procedure to ensure staff are made aware of when their PC needs to be available, with as much notice as possible (even an email will suffice).

If you have a member of staff who is particularly prone to obstructing access to their PC (it happens), it might be a good idea to accompany the consultant to that desk to facilitate a smooth handover.

Ensuring the team is on board with accommodating your third-party tech support will ensure prompt completion of all the tasks, at far less cost.

Distractions

We've all been in the dentist chair, listening to the surgeon casually chat away with the nurse whilst simultaneously extending dental forceps towards our molars. Is it just me, or have you actually wanted to yell out – focus for heaven sakes!

No matter what our profession, and however capable we might be at multi-tasking, there really is no way anyone can genuinely concentrate on the task at hand if someone else is 'bending their ear off' – even if the conversation is topical. Focus is diminished by distraction.

In my early days as a systems administrator, I would shadow the third party IT professional in order to learn as much about his skills as possible. An incredibly astute and capable man, he made it quite clear from the offset that I should remember that his primary focus was to get the job done. He emphasized that this would require some intense deliberation on his part.

In order to avoid distraction, he respectfully asked that I observe in silence, waiting until he had concluded his work before bombarding him with a million questions.

As I later discovered for myself, resolving IT support issues does require a huge degree of focus and concentration - especially when the incident is major or time-critical. So if you have appointed an IT specialist and they have attended site to address the problem, be mindful to allow time for discussion, as well as time for quiet deliberation.

That's not to say that you should leave them entirely to their own devices, especially if you wish to be kept in the loop every step of the way. If it is necessary for you to shadow them, respect the space needed for them to gather their thoughts and scope out a plan of action.

The most experienced consultants will have adopted their own unique method when deploying a solution to a problem, but if asked to empower another with the skills needed to resolve the same issue in-house, the consultant will probably modify his approach in order to effectively educate his delegate.

Either way, facilitating uninterrupted time to the consultant will pave the way to a more speedy solution.

Here today gone tomorrow

As an expert in multiple Microsoft applications, I have always deployed solutions for my clients 'out of the box'. That is, I implement exactly as Microsoft intended. Not only does this allow for a more reliable installation, it ensures that my clients are not cornered into a scenario where only I can support their system.

With so many millions of Microsoft engineers skilled at managing the products I deploy, my clients are liberated and able to seek support from anyone.

These days, taking on software applications that cannot be supported by the masses is a risky strategy.

Occasionally, small businesses struggle to find an off-shelf solution that effectively meets their IT needs. In this instance it may be necessary to adopt a bespoke application that can be developed manually to meet their exacting needs. However, due diligence should be applied in order to avoid being exposed to excessive charges and a product that absolutely no one can support.

I recently encountered a client who had spent years developing a bespoke application with a third-party programmer. The client was entirely happy with the way the application had evolved, even though he felt vulnerable knowing that he had inadvertently placed all his eggs in one basket (by allowing a one man band to build this solution for him).

Sadly his worst nightmare was realized when the developer went out of business, leaving the client without any potential for further development or ongoing support.

There was no user manual or development notes, and the product was so unique and complex that it was virtually impossible for any third-party to pick up the reins and offer a level of support even remotely resembling the work of the original programmer.

The upshot was that the client had to abandon this product altogether and start again from scratch. He was forced to write off the entire value of his original investment.

Fortunately, he was able to find a suitable off-shelf solution. With a small amount of customization, he was relieved to discover the replacement actually did the job as effectively as his original product - for much less money.

Beware of bespoke solutions. If they are absolutely critical, ensure the product can be supported by any other third party - no matter what happens to the software developer.

Chapter 5
Do It Yourself

Prepare the Goods

Purchasing new equipment is an inevitable part of small business IT growth and stability. Unfortunately the costs associated with new equipment are not limited to the initial purchase. Whether replacing old PCs or adding new ones to an existing network, you are likely to need tech support to assist in their setup.

If you are working with an IT support company, it is likely you will invite them to set the computers up for you. If the consultant you appoint is supplying the goods, delivery and installation is likely to occur on the same day. However, you might prefer to order in the equipment from the manufacturer directly, then contact tech support when they arrive.

Either way, there is an opportunity for you to save time on installation costs. Here's how.

First, consider the positioning of the computers. If the new computer is not intended as a replacement for an existing one, check that there are sufficient power outputs at the desk where the new PC will reside. It would be a good idea to organize some extension leads or surge protector ahead of the day of installation too. A computer will typically require two power connections, so a four-way extension would be a safe bet.

Also give thought to the network connection. You are likely to want the new computers to be joined to your existing network. Unless it is a laptop being installed, your PC will not come with wireless capability as standard, so you will need to ensure you have a network point nearby. If in any doubt as to what you are looking for, call tech support ahead of their visit to discuss the prerequisites.

Another way to save time and money on new equipment installation is to be on hand to unpack the equipment. The time it takes to unbox a PC, position it on the desk, plug it in and turn it on takes around 10 minutes. If you have ordered 6, that's one hour you can shave off tech support time if you assist with the unpacking, so consider unboxing the goods before the support person arrives. If the consultant is bringing them on the day of install, shadow them with the unboxing. Once they have shown you how to unbox one, ask the internally appointed 'Systems Administrator' or other member of staff to assist with the unboxing.

YouTube has thousands of video showing users how to unbox devices, from iPhones and printers to washing machines and hoovers. As these videos demonstrate there is nothing specialist about it - just be sure to keep everything together and do not discard CDs or manuals as these need to be kept safe.

Whatever the device, ensuring that it is in an easily accessible state will mean the IT professional can get cracking right away - which has to be better for your pocket.

Consultants on a premium rate will not object to opening boxes, but this can be done by anyone so go ahead and muck in. Don't be afraid to take over this task whilst they progress with other technical issues. A reputable consultant will prefer using their time efficiently, and will respect your objective to save money.

Fragile Beware

When a computer is shipped from the manufacturer, it is securely wrapped in a heavy duty box, shrouded in polystyrene and encased in bubble wrap. It might also be labelled "this way up". The purpose is to ensure safe delivery but in my experience, the belief that the equipment is "fragile" may linger in some computer owners long after the packaging has been discarded.

There is a common misconception that, once installed, a personal computer should not be moved as doing so might damage it. With so many wires and connections to consider, it's easy to understand how a less confident computer user might be concerned about causing a catastrophic failure with only themselves to blame.

Of course all electronic items must respected, but they are considerably more robust than you think.

Whether the computer is used for home or work, there will invariably come a time when the entire caboodle needs to be moved or relocated.

The good news is that disconnecting, relocating, and reconnecting a computer does not require an IT specialist. By following some simple steps, even the most feint-hearted could relocate a computer.

1. Be sure the desk you are relocating to has sufficient mains power outlets and network points if required. Check this before you move the computer to save yourself the hassle of having to move it back again.

2. Take a photograph of the back of the computer. This will give you a snapshot of the exact cable connections. Count how many cables you have connected and write it down. If you are still anxious about unplugging the cables, try labelling the cables and mark the back of the computer with a corresponding label for each cable.

3. Shut the computer down before you start. It is perfectly safe to remove the cables in any order, but I usually leave the mains cable until last. When removing the cable, be sure to look for any screws that might be holding the cable in place. There might also be plastic tabs that need to be pinched in as you ease out the cable. The rule is - if it doesn't pull out easily, check for a screw or tab which could be stopping it.

4. As you pull the cable out be sure to pull it out straight – do not apply any pressure down or up or you may damage the connections.

You are now ready to reposition the computer. There is no order of things when reconnecting either – just be sure you get them all in before attempting to turn on the computer.

The chances of you needing technical support are very slim, but even if something is not right and you need help, think of how much time has been saved on expensive specialist support by physically moving the computer ahead of their visit.

Don't be afraid to move computer equipment yourself. This does not require a specialist, just some common sense and some planning and preparation.

Escalation

Technology moves so fast. Even the most common applications are prone to application failure, halting productivity and leaving end users exasperated.

A wide variety of issues will undoubtedly be handled by your systems administrator or third party IT support, but if your company operates one or more specialist applications, there may be times when approaching your familiar tech support company may not be the best place to start.

Many specialist applications, such as Sage Accounts, are incredibly unique and complex, so when an application error appears in a product of this kind, escalation to a specialist may be required.

Specialist products are invariably offered with support cover, which gives you and your team direct access to specialist support. Sadly though, specialist support can be expensive so some business owners choose not to obtain specialist support cover and instead place the onus on the existing IT support guy.

Dealing with Microsoft application errors is one thing, but even the most competent of tech support professionals will recommend you obtain support directly from the manufacturer of your specialist product. He or she may be versed at installing that program - even setting up and training the users, but when it comes to addressing issues that are inherent within the application itself, your technical support is likely to recommend that you contact the manufacturer directly, or even offer to call on your behalf.

It is a false economy to throw caution to the wind and adopt specialist applications without specialist support. The objective of support is to achieve a solution as quickly and as efficiently as possible, so whilst tech support might be willing to have a stab at fixing the problem within a specialist application, it stands to reason that he is unlikely to expedite a speedy solution.

If you have already paid for specialist support, in the event of an error with that application, this should be your first port of call. Avoid calling your regular tech support and asking them to call the specialist support on your behalf. Paying a third party to call a third party is an unnecessary waste of money. Most specialist product providers offer excellent support services - they are versed at successfully communicating with even the most nervous of computer users.

Once you have escalated the matter with specialist support, you might feel that some of the recommended steps to fixing the problem are over and above your own skill sets, in which case this is the perfect time to refer back to third-party assistance if necessary.

A reputable IT support company will encourage you to involve specialist support - before getting into any chargeable time to assist.

Right people

Business owners undoubtedly have a duty of care to invest wisely, and avoid unnecessary costs wherever possible by adopting a DIY approach. However, it may still be necessary to call upon specialist support for certain aspects of the project.

Bloody Computers

A business owner was planning to relocate premises 120 miles from his original site. He was loathe to pay the premium his tech support quoted to travel such distance, so he elected to take the matter into his own hands. He decided to move his server and six computers himself.

Unfortunately things did not go according to plan, and in spite his best efforts he was at a loss as to why the computers could not connect to the network once he had finished setting them up in the new building.

As a local IT service provider he contacted me following a recommendation. He explained over the phone that the situation was critical. His company was unable to trade, his staff were idle and he had no one else to turn to.

Ordinarily, I am usually loathe to dive straight into a supporting role without first having an understanding of the setup. However, given his situation I offered an emergency same-day visit.

I was greeted with a warm welcome and promptly given a tour of the IT systems. Everything looked in order and actually he had done a great job setting everything up. At first glance, it seemed there was little for me to do. But the computers were not connecting, and it was quickly evident why.

There was not one single network point in the building. Network points are sockets on the wall that computers connect to. This enables file sharing and internet access - without a network connection, the computers are isolated from one another.

When I explained the problem, I was astonished at his angry outburst:

"Nobody told me I needed network cabling - not even you when we spoke on the phone. I take it you will get it done today?"

If a site survey had been arranged ahead of the relocation, I could have proactively advised that network cabling is a specialist job and requires the services of a data cabling company.

Although a little ruffled by the accusation that this was somehow my fault I was still keen to help, so I provided some lengths of lose network cabling as a temporary solution and within 10 minutes I had his network up and running.

Unfortunately, the client went on to express his disappointment that I had not tacked the cable to the skirting board. I carry many things in my technical toolkit, but a hammer is not one of them, so in response I recommended appointing a handyman who would charge considerably less than an IT specialist.

Even if I had been able to install structured cabling, or had been adequately equipped to tack the cables to the skirting, I had been appointed as an IT consultant and support specialist - so undertaking these duties at consultancy rates would not have been a cost-effective way for him to utilize my time.

Had he scoped out his plans and sought a second opinion on the readiness of the new building, structured cabling could have been installed and he wouldn't have needed a temporary supply of network cabling or a handyman to hide them.

Be proactive and involve third party specialists ahead of your IT projects. This will ensure you appoint the right person for the job, at the appropriate rate.

Chapter 6
Don't Be Hasty

Out with the Old

Technology is moving so fast that, for many computer users, it is a job to keep up. The pace of change is particularly apparent in the look and feel of software such as Microsoft Windows - where the version changes bear no resemblance to the last, once again rendering them wildly unfamiliar to the user.

As a result of rapid technological advances, computers have become disposal items. But can we really justify the recurring costs of replacing equipment?

Calculating the true cost of ownership is impossible, because we cannot predict how long a computer will remain in operation. All we can do is hope it lasts as long as possible.

Some of my clients have a strict policy of replacing a computer when it reaches the end of its 3 year warranty. Others prefer to wait until it is on its last legs. But whether it just scrapes by its warranty period or outlives your delightful old great aunt, how soon should a computer be replaced?

The fact that a computer is 'old' is simply not enough to justify replacing it.

If a PC is operational, and enables the user to carry out the tasks required of it, why incur the cost?

Some unscrupulous vendors might insist you have no choice for the reasons highlighted below, but the counter-argument cannot be easily ignored:

Outdated operating system. You may be running an old version of Windows that Microsoft no longer supports. However, in some environments keeping the PC in service is still entirely plausible. You need to ask yourself where and how the computer is used. Unsupported operating systems are rendered vulnerable by the absence of windows updates (these updates repair security flaws). However, if web browsing is minimal, or limited to just a handful of websites, the risk is low, provided other security measures are maintained (up-to-date anti-virus software, frequent servicing, and user vigilance).

New software. Many of the latest software applications are created and tested on the most recent versions of Windows. Should this be the case, it is still not a given that the computer should be replaced. There is a potential for it to be upgraded to the latest version.

Minimum Spec. The specification of your PC may not be high enough to accommodate certain software applications. If your computer or laptop is less than three years old, it is highly likely that it has the potential to be upgraded with additional memory or storage. Upgrading an existing computer is undoubtedly the most cost-effective way of extending the life and functionality of your computer. Even a computer that is running slow has potential for a renewed lease of life.

Slow computers can also be rebuilt in order to restore their performance to their original shipped-state.

Whatever the age of your computer, or status of your warranty, maximize your investment and dismiss the erroneous suggestion that a replacement is the only option.

Check out our compatibility checker here:
www.bloodycomputersbook.com/resources

Mac versus PC

Although I have supported Microsoft products for over 30 years, I completely and utterly adore Apple technology. The architecture of a Mac is very different than the PC. It is sleek, captivating and undoubtedly provides one of the most unique and inspiring experiences to any end user who has the pleasure of operating one.

In my capacity as an IT consultant, my clients often ask if they should invest in a Mac. My response is the same for everyone - it depends entirely on what you want to do with it.

Standard PCs running Microsoft software are common in the workplace and provide a great platform for team collaboration. The Microsoft suite of applications such as Windows, Excel, and Word is widely recognized and supported by the masses, and provides a friendly interface for the user.

Apple computers are frequently utilized in a creative environment such as design studios or publishing houses. Mac is a great publishing tool and lends itself perfectly to multi-media activity.

Both deliver great solutions - but there are many things to consider when contemplating the introduction of a Mac Computer into your existing Windows environment:

What is its purpose? There is no doubt than an iMac makes for wonderful eye-candy. It boasts the sleekest and most appealing design of any computer I have ever seen, but what exactly will you use it for? Be sure your objective for acquiring one is for functional reasons and not just visual.

Support Costs. Whilst there is an abundance of Windows engineers on hand to offer assistance with all things Microsoft, in comparison, experienced Mac engineers are like gold dust. As such, Mac support is in greater demand so it will result in a much higher charge for support services.

End user skills. A classic mistake is to assume that experienced Windows users will find the transition to Mac a simple one that can be self-taught. This is rarely the case. The architecture is so very different so you must be prepared to arrange for specialist training if you are to fully utilize the features available to a Mac user.

Before launching ahead with your acquisition, check your IT support team provide Mac support, and confirm the costs. Scope out your requirements with a trusted third party, and remember to ask someone you know in a similar environment what benefits this device bring them when compared to a conventional PC.

When it comes to the workplace, business owners still invest in PCs because they are cheaper to buy, easier to support, and widely recognized by the majority of staff. Mac users do experience far fewer viruses and malware than PC users, but at the end of the day, companies need to factor in the total cost of ownership.

The Mac might be a thing of pristine beauty, but before investing, look at the bigger picture and do your due diligence.

Think before you click

We are all wary of salesmen knocking our front door at home or in the workplace - trying to sell us something. No matter what they are selling, most of us know not to trust them, let alone invite them in. The sad truth though is if they visit enough doors, they will make a sale eventually.

When it comes to computer viruses, the same cautious approach you would take to a stranger at your door should be applied to a stranger in your mailbox - do not trust them and do not let them in.

When a computer user clicks on an attachment or link that arrives within an email, the user is executing and essentially 'allowing' the computer to perform the actions behind that link. The link may be nothing more annoying than a redirect to a website of products you have no desire to purchase. But in more extreme cases, you may inadvertently unleash malicious activity onto your PC.

Some of this activity can be downright nasty. It can cause your important documentation to become encrypted, with a ransom being levied against you for the safe recovery of your data. Equally disastrous, the infection may corrupt the operating system, rendering the computer unstable.

I have never suffered from a virus on my computer - not because I have the most advanced anti-virus protection known to mankind, but because there is no substitute for user vigilance. Agreed, I am probably slightly more skilled at recognizing a suspicious attachment or a dodgy link, but I can vouch for dozens of clients who literally have never exposed their computers to a virus, simply by being exceptionally vigilant.

It is not just emails from strangers you should be wary of though. You might receive an email from a trusted source that, without your knowledge, contains malicious links or attachments.

You may trust this email at first glance since you know the sender, but take a closer look - do the contents reflect the usual tone or approach of that particular contact? If it is incredibly unlikely that your friend would use the term "howdy", then you can pretty much guess the email is not what it claims to be. It is entirely possible that your trusted contact has had his or her mailbox hijacked, leading to the submission of a harmful email to everyone in their address book - without their knowledge.

Another place where malicious content can find its way onto your computer is from web browsing. Web searches are the primary source of illegitimate downloads because the user unwittingly trusts the search results. The top hit is not always the right hit - be sure to scroll down the list of results and target only those who have a domain name that legitimately represents the product or provider you were searching for.

Be internet savvy - open attachments and downloads only if they are from a trustworthy person or company. If you were not expecting the email, take a moment to check that the content truly reflects the spirit of the sender.

If in any doubt, delete the email and pick up the phone to the sender - it is less costly and time-consuming than recovering from a computer virus.

Action through Inaction

Even the most confident of computer users may panic when an email bounces as 'undelivered'. An email 'non-delivery report'

Bloody Computers

is often hard to decipher, leaving the user doubting the integrity of their mail flow.

Whatever you do, do not adjust your settings. Knee-jerk reactions like this can only make matters worse. Unless you have received confirmation of new setting from your internet service provider, making changes to them in response to a non-delivery report may seriously impact upon your ability to resolve the issue later.

There are multiple reasons why an email might bounce – best practice would be to check for these things ahead of any call to tech support:-

Check that the email address you have used is accurate. A full stop or incorrect spelling may be the cause of the send failure. Check the spelling and try sending a new email from scratch.

Ask the recipient to email you. Ask the person you are emailing to send you an email. Once you receive it, try replying to it.

Ask a colleague to try the same address. Ask a colleague from your organization to also try emailing the recipient you are having trouble reaching, and ask them to share the outcome with you.

The non-delivery report you receive will explain the reason for the bounce and you may be able to glean some clues by looking for some telling paragraphs or phrases within the report itself. Often these reports state things like "recipient mailbox is full" or "invalid address". Taking the time to check this information can save you in support costs.

Is this the only non-delivery report you have received? If it is, it is most likely a one off and may resolve itself if you wait a couple of hours then retry. It is entirely possible that the recipient is having issues, or your own internet service provider is having problems. If you try sending the email again 24 hours later, there is every chance the issue will have resolved itself.

Action through inaction is sometimes the cheapest cure.

Of course, if you have received multiple non-delivery reports, you may still need to escalate the matter to tech support. Be sure to share the information you have gathered, and provide a copy of the non-delivery report. All of this information is crucial to their investigation, and will help expedite a fix.

Chapter 7
The Unscrupulous

Caution to the wind

Business owners have plenty of IT consultants to choose from - there are literally millions of them out there, all vying for your business. Most are reliable, hardworking and trustworthy but, like any industry, there will always be a handful of unsavory types in their midst - unscrupulous to the core, intent on deceiving in order to maximize their income.

If you have read my earlier chapters, you will have successfully navigated around the pirates of the IT world. You can enjoy a sense of reassurance that you are not one of the poor victims who find themselves in the clutches of such menacing bad apples.

The most destructive of the IT villains are those who throw caution to the wind. Frequently out of their depth, they will not care because it will only ever be at the expense of the client. Even when they finds themself in the thick of disaster, they have the ability to talk themself out of the mess.

I came across such a character through a former client, after they had moved to another part of the country and subsequently sourced someone local to take over their IT support.

The newly appointed consultant quickly recommended replacing their old server. Unfortunately he did not bother to mention that he had no previous experience of migrating data from one server to another. Instead he decided to give it a go anyway, with disastrous consequences - his inexperience led to a catastrophic annihilation of the client's original server when his attempts to migrate failed.

He might have held on to a shred of integrity had he just admitted his failings, but instead he delivered the now entirely unstable server to a friend on account that "his friend knew a little bit more about servers." A further 48 hours was wasted, trying to recover the situation without success. He finally conceded to defeat and relinquished control of the original server, which was subsequently shipped back to my control so the recovery process could begin.

The conduct of this individual was both selfish and unprofessional, yet he still had the audacity to invoice the client for the time he AND his friend spent trying to recover the server.

Needless to say the client did not pay.

Recommendations are the safest, most cost-effective way to secure third-party IT support - but it needs to be from someone who has implemented a like for like solution. Where possible, ask for other testimonials from the consultant, and follow up on them before embarking on any major projects or development work.

Fruitless Effort

Your computer has died from what appears to be a catastrophic hardware failure. Your warranty has expired and you need to recover the files from the hard drive. You wish you had made time to back up the files – you had always intended to but it kept getting put to the back of the list.

Even with limited knowledge, you may feel justified investing a small amount of time trying to fix the problem yourself – even if you recognize this may prove futile. There is the obvious 'turn it off and on again' – always worth a try. You might even bravely attempt to swap out some of the components, switch a few cables, perform a google search for solutions and make a few calls to friends.

Unfortunately you realize this has all been a fruitless effort leaving you overwhelmed and defeated.

Investing your own time to attempt the recovery of your computer is one thing, but when you appoint a third party, you are likely to incur charges on the clock. Of course, you probably will not object to paying for those repairs to get your computer back in working order, but what happens if the cost to repair is prohibitive?

I have heard countless examples of unscrupulous consultants charging more than the value of the computer for the item to be fixed - and in some cases an unreasonable charge has been levied even though the device could not be returned in a repaired state.

Data recovery is a lucrative business - tech support will know that your priority is likely to be the resurrection of your valuable data. This gives rise to the opportunity for leverage - pay heavily or you will not get your data back.

Before releasing your equipment for repair, agree on your priorities and confirm the costs.

If you call upon a reputable and respectable provider, they will first help you decide your priorities. In many cases it would be the safe recovery of the data. The price to recover data could then be agreed on ahead of the work – enabling you to make an informed decision. However, if repairing the equipment is more important, ask for a fixed fee for diagnostics. The objective at the end of it is to be given a quote for replacement parts – not a hefty bill for futile effort and no PC to show for it.

Before calling upon assistance, take into account the age and value of the computer, and ask yourself how much you are prepared to invest toward the repair of old equipment. If the repairs cost more than a replacement, put your money towards a new computer.

Critical errors

We have all experienced the "critical error" message that pops up on our computer or laptop from time to time. Anyone familiar with the event logs on a computer will know that the words 'error' and 'critical' make an all too frequent appearance, even on the healthiest of computers.

So how important are these alerts?

Microsoft uses the term 'critical' to alert you to important updates. These updates improve the stability and security of your PC. The word 'error' is used to indicate the failure of certain functions. The vast majority of these errors are simply background failures which often have absolutely no bearing on the performance of your computer.

The truth is, the word critical is just another word for 'important'. The intention of the word critical is to make the computer user aware that, at that moment in time, something important occurred or needs to occur. This does not mean the computer is about to suffer catastrophic failure.

Taken out of context, you could be forgiven for believing that these error messages suggest your equipment has suffered from a disaster and requires immediate attention. Sadly, this is how the criminal fraternity can attempt to deceive you.

Unfortunately, scammers use these error messages to gain your trust in the hope of getting access to your computer. Here's how they do it:

You receive a phone call from someone claiming to be from Microsoft. They politely declare your computer has submitted error reports and they want to help. If you don't believe them, they will talk you through how to open the event logs where you will find error messages. Once they have gained your trust, they will offer a free fix, or charge a nominal fee for support - all you have to do is give them access to your computer with a few simple steps. Once connected, they will pretend to fix the issues but in the background they will scanning your files for credit card details - which you may have innocently saved to a notepad or word document on your hard drive.

Be aware, Microsoft will never ever call you to offer to fix your computer. Unless the call is from your officially appointed tech support, never give remote access to someone who you did not call personally. Never save passwords or credit card information in a standard document.

Respectable IT technicians will refer to your event logs to determine the health of your computer, but they are far from the only method used to accurately diagnose issues with your PC.

For more information on safe storage of passwords, visit www.bloodycomputersbook.com/resources

Software Piracy

All software on your computer has a license associated with it. In the case of Microsoft Windows for example, the license essentially confirms your entitlement to use the software and one license per computer is required.

Licensing was much simpler in the early days of the personal computer, but with the advent of software piracy, it has become a stricter and much more complicated process for computer manufacturers and owners alike.

Sadly, this does not prevent the scammers from scamming, as one of my most recent clients discovered.

I first met this particular client when he parted company with his existing IT provider. As part of the initial introduction, I performed a site survey with the objective of gathering information regarding his setup.

He had 10 computers, and as the survey unfolded so too did the problems.

The first challenge was that the client had no receipts for the purchase of the equipment. He was keen to know the age of the PCs. If a computer is supplied from a branded manufacturer, it is usually possible to confirm the exact date it was made. Unfortunately, the computers this client owned were clones - that is, they were built by the previous IT support guy. Consequently, they had no brand or badge, and there was no shipping information adhered to the side. In this particular scenario it was impossible to accurately determine the age of each computer.

The next challenge was much more sinister - the guy who built these computers had re-used the first Windows license and installed it on all ten computers. Not only is this an infringement of trademark and copyright laws, it is a criminal offence on the part of the system builder.

More importantly, this left the client in breach of Microsoft licensing laws. It seemed likely he had paid the full license cost per PC, but had been sold only one valid license.

I hate to be the bearer of bad news so I did not relish sharing my findings with the client. However, it turns out he had called upon my services immediately after he had learned that his so-called IT guy had been charged with fraud and sent to prison.

Needless to say our first priority was to purchase genuine licenses for this client. This was achieved by the costly replacement of the cloned computers for genuine, manufacturer-supplied computers for all 10 users - an expensive and very harsh lesson for this poor unsuspecting client.

When purchasing equipment be sure the provider supplies valid and genuine certification or other documentation to prove the validity of any licenses.

Chapter 8
Potential Hazards

Beware of bargains

Everyone loves a bargain, but when it comes to a new computer or laptop, how do you know you have genuinely acquired a high spec device at a discounted rate, and not just a cheaply made computer?

There is a classic buying mistake made when purchasing replacement equipment - and that is having high expectations and a low budget.

One of my clients recommended me to a close acquaintance who needed advice on a replacement laptop. She had already decided that her old laptop was slow and tatty and had set herself a budget for a new one. We discussed her requirements for this new laptop, but it was quickly evident that her budget did not match her exacting needs. She needed high performance to accommodate the specific software she was using, and she needed lightweight for ease of transportation. I explained that her budget would not buy her a suitable replacement and I encouraged her to spend a little more.

I also warned her that new laptops currently come with Windows 8 pre-installed, so unless she was comfortable to move away from the familiar features of Windows 7, she should request a downgrade with her purchase.

I did not hear from this client again until several weeks later, when she called to ask for assistance with performance issues on her new laptop.

It materialized she had found a bargain buy that allegedly met all her needs, so she purchased it. Sadly, her new laptop was far from ideal and she confessed to being disappointed from day one. The so-called deal did not permit her the flexibility of a downgrade, so she had to agree to have Windows 8. With no previous experience, she felt she had wasted precious time getting to grips with it. The new laptop was also slower than the old one and she hadn't realized the deal did not include a three-year warranty. Instead she got just one year.

With the benefit of hindsight, this client realized that had she been a little more flexible with her budget, she would have benefitted from more buying power. The options on bargain deals are often fixed, so if you want to factor in something unique to your exacting requirements, avoid purchasing a deal that has been manufactured for the masses.

Don't be afraid to ask for advice from different sources and compare the answers you get. Some retailers list the key specifications of each product clearly, which can be a good place to start.

Your appointed consultant will know the things you should consider before making a purchase. If they understand your infrastructure or requirements, they can provide you with the best advice.

Cheap Imitations

The cost of computers has reduced massively over the years. When they were first on sale in the shops, it was rare to find anything under £1000. These days, they are throwaway items, but do you really know what you are getting when you part with your cash, or are you likely to regret being seduced by a bargain at a later date?

There are several things to consider when purchasing a computer:

What do you want to use it for?
What is your budget?
Where do you plan to purchase it from?

Whatever your requirements, there is one simple rule. You get what you pay for. If the purchase price is cheap, the components inside are probably cheap too.

There is a lot to be said for purchasing your equipment directly from the manufacturer. I have always personally recommended Dell products. I use them both in-house and for clients. I am not a reseller for Dell, so I have no financial motive for recommending their products - I do so simply because I trust the quality and the service provided at reasonable rates. The rates are low due to the fact that they are mass-produced. They also have a reputation to uphold, so it is in their best interest to provide equipment that is manufactured to a high standard.

The DIY system builder is likely to imply that he can build you a computer at significantly lower rates than the likes of Dell. The trouble is, without knowing one end of a motherboard from another, you have no way of vouching for the quality of the components used to build a computer from scratch.

This provides the unscrupulous system builder plenty of unchallenged opportunity to buy cheap components and sell them at a bumper price.

Cheap components are more likely to fail than those supplied from a respectable, branded manufacturer.

Even if assembled with expert precision, there is usually something unsavory about one or more of the components - from its flimsy case to the low spec CD. And then there is the issue with the warranty. I know of several instances where a 'homemade' computer was sold with 'one year warranty'. When a part failed, instead of honoring a warranty repair the system builder referred the owner directly to the manufacturer of the faulty part. This is both unreasonable and futile, since the manufacturer will expect you to produce a receipt demonstrating the purchase of that individual component (which you will not have since you did not purchase the part directly).

Some of the larger manufacturers also provide their consumers with a driver site, where latest versions of the software that help to keep your computers components running efficiently can be downloaded free of charge. DIY system builders are unlikely to itemize the make and model of components inside your computer, let alone invest in the development of a website to facilitate access to the latest drivers.

The safest way to buy is to ask an IT support person, who knows your setup inside out, what they would recommend. This will ensure your expectations are managed and the correct budget set to match your needs. Choose from a reputable and recommended provider and avoid self-build solutions wherever possible.

Slow Broadband

As humans, we are hardwired to want things – now! We need instant gratification without delay or deferment. The rapid evolution of information technology has fulfilled those demands by giving us high spec equipment and 'always on' devices. But when it comes to high-speed broadband, Britain is falling behind. Poor speeds and limited scope for upgrade potential is the Achilles heel for many business owners.

The problem is worse in rural areas, but even businesses in towns and cities struggle with slow broadband speeds. This can play a critical role in the success of any organization.

There are several things you should check though, before writing off all hope of superfast broadband. With so many variables affecting the performance of any existing service, frequent checks should be performed in order to ensure you achieve the speeds your broadband provider intended:

Has your broadband always been slow? If your broadband used to run super quick but has worsened or lagged over time, there may be an underlying issue that with some investigation could be identified and resolved. You may have a fault on the line broadband is provisioned on (unless it takes the service down completely, line faults frequently go undetected).

There may be a virus on one of your computers. Malware and virus activity can have a huge impact on the broadband bandwidth because it essentially hogs the service.

The important thing to bear in mind is that, if broadband seems slower than it once was before, it would be a good idea to call in tech support or your broadband provider to check things out.

Understand your Speeds. Do you know what broadband speed you are paying for, and how that compares to what you are actually getting? Your broadband provider can confirm this over the phone and they will be able to talk you through how to run a speed check. If the two do not marry, this may highlight issues with the service or with the broadband equipment. If the router is ageing, ask your provider or tech support to provide a replacement. Ask neighbors what speeds they get too. This will help confirm whether the issue is isolated to your network or with your broadband service provider.

Ask for an upgrade. This may not be available, but unless you ask it is unlikely your broadband provider will upgrade you automatically or even notify you when one becomes available. Shop around for other providers too, as some may be able to improve your speeds by offering you alternative products not currently available from your existing provider.

Are you connected wirelessly? Switching to a wired connection will improve the stability of your connection and can improve your speeds. Environmental issues (such as thick walls) can interfere with your wireless network so establish a connection with an ethernet cable where possible. Also check that your wireless broadcast is encrypted with a secure access key to ensure valuable bandwidth is not being used by any neighboring property cheeky enough to hop onto your broadband service for free.

Software Downloads. Avoid downloading large software packages over a network where other users are sharing broadband. If you have poor speeds, downloading software packages will take up valuable bandwidth and will impact directly on the connection speeds for other users. If you need tech support to install the software, ask them to download any software onto USB from their own office, or do this yourself from home. Installation can then be carried out from the USB device.

Wherever possible, do due diligence of the broadband speeds before you move your business into new premises. Do not make decisions based on promises from providers as they have no way of guaranteeing timelines for the provision of new services.

Do not just accept slow broadband speeds. Refer to the above tips to ensure you are running at the best performance levels possible.

Test your broadband speeds with our free speed checker.
Visit www.bloodycomputersbook.com/resources

Inevitable updates

Windows updates are enhancements to the software that is running on your computer. They are provided completely free of charge, and can prevent or fix problems. Updates improve the security of the computer and can also enhance performance.

Microsoft recommends that these updates be applied automatically, so that security and other important or recommended updates can be installed as they become available.

Sadly though, the process for ensuring the successful deployment of these updates is extremely ambiguous, and many end users are unaware of the prerequisites required of them personally, as the user of that computer.

The first thing you should know is that these updates are often presented in linear batches. Each batch might contain multiple updates, but subsequent batches will not run until the previous batch has been applied correctly. Unfortunately, a significant number of updates require that the computer be rebooted - or even powered off and on again - in order to install correctly.

If a computer user finds it more convenient to leave the computer on overnight and does not turn his or computer off on a frequent basis, it is entirely possible that he is unwittingly preventing the completion of pending updates. This will create a bottleneck scenario and may lead to the computer falling behind with these important enhancements.

Update alerts can be enabled to prompt the end user but in my experience, many users doubt the validity or origin of such prompts and as such they may unwittingly decline to let them run.

There is a difference between updates pending a restart, and updates pending a shutdown. A restart does not turn off the power of the computer, a shutdown does.

The user cannot easily tell if updates are pending a restart - it is only when clicking the restart button that these updates announce themselves. However, a Windows 7 user can tell if updates are pending a computer shutdown, because an exclamation mark will appear on the shutdown button itself.

If you are trying to save on IT support costs, avoid leaving windows updates to tech support. Instead, ask your consultant to confirm that automatic updates are enabled on every computer (and disable notification too). Then encourage your staff to restart their computers once per day, and power off the computer at least once per week. Lunchtime is a good opportunity, or at the end of the day. This will help maintain the computers and it will give the employee a sense of ownership and responsibility for their own equipment. Furthermore, it will ensure that delays (and potentially additional charges) are not incurred when IT support performs routine or maintenance work.

For more information on windows updates, visit www.bloodycomputersbook.com/resources

Bespoke Solutions

If your business is growing rapidly, technical development will be crucial to your survival. When it comes to investing in the all-singing-all-dancing software solution, how do you pick the best solution to ensure your evolution and growth?

Software packages are available in two flavors:

Off-Shelf: this is the 'ready-to-go' solution, designed to get you up and running the moment the product is installed.

Bespoke: This is where the software is designed from scratch by a developer, with a view to creating something that meets your exacting needs.

Off-shelf solutions are by far the most common. They are mass-produced, so the price will be much lower. They are available immediately and invariably accessible on CD or internet download. Training costs are low too, since off-shelf products are frequently packed full of existing training equipment and learning courses.

Another advantage to off-shelf solutions is they can be supported in the community because they are so widely recognized. Support consultants will have either used these products themselves, or encountered the software on many of their client sites. And if that isn't enough, there are always books, articles and online support forums providing advice to help resolve any issues.

With so much going for off-shelf products, it's hard to see why anyone would want to opt for a bespoke solution, but there is one main reason - compromise.

Off-shelf solutions are based on the theory that one size fits all. Even those products that offer a degree of customization are limited in terms of flexibility. Clients who are not willing to accept the absence of certain features will need to turn to custom-made solutions.

Bespoke software will indulge you in a tailor-made solution in order meet your exacting requirements, whilst ensuring flexibility for your company's nuances. A bespoke solution also provides a competitive advantage, since your providers will not have access to the same software.

However, there are disadvantages too:

- Ongoing development will result in higher costs, which (dependent upon the complexity of the product) could go on for many months or even years.
- Implementation will take much longer and staff training will need to be ongoing.
- There is a risk that the developer could disappear at any time and you may be left with intellectual property that no other vendor can support.

One of my own clients suffered massive losses when his software developer went into receivership. His particular bespoke application had been built up by the developer over several years. Sadly, the developer had treated it like a work in progress, and as such, had not provided any system or training manuals before pulling the plug on the service. When later calculating the losses, the client realized he had invested 20 times more than the cost of an off-shelf solution.

If not managed properly, bespoke solutions will become the journey from hell, with charges at every stop and no real fixed arrival time. Before committing, scope out the boundaries by agreeing phases to the implementation, and consider the implications on the project if the developer were unable to complete the job.

Chapter 9
Knowledge is Power

Windows downgrade

Microsoft introduced major changes to the operating system platform when they introduced Windows 8. This particular version included a new style interface for use with touch screens for both laptops and tablets. It was intended to improve its user experience but it had a mixed reception and was widely criticised for being difficult and confusing to learn.

Business owners were finding flaws in Windows 8. Notwithstanding the incredibly unfamiliar colour-tiled start screen, they preferred the efficiency and functionality of previous versions.

New computers typically come preloaded with the latest versions of windows. However, buyers who want to avoid the hassle of training staff on how to use a new interface can opt for a downgrade against certain models. Before requesting a downgrade, there are some things you need to know that could save you time and money at a later date.

First, if the Supplier offers you downgrade rights, ask them to install the downgrade for you. This will save you the hassle of sourcing installation CDs yourself as these are not usually provided with your downgraded computer. In addition, asking the manufacturer to do this means they will be able to manage the reactivation process for you, which means calling Microsoft for a single-use activation code.

Second, be aware that not all computers on sale are compatible for downgrade. If the system has been built specifically for the latest version of windows, you might be limited on the range of models available so you will need to discuss the options with your supplier. The important thing is, once you have agreed to the spec, ensure they do the downgrade for you.

When the computer arrives, you will need to create a recovery CD yourself – this is because downgrade PCs and laptops will be shipped with a recovery disk for the newer version of windows. If you ever need to rebuild your computer, and you wish to stick with your older version you must create some recovery CDs. For this you will need several blank read-writable discs or an external USB hard drive, and 1-2 hours spare whilst the recovery disks are built.

There are many possible scenarios which may lead to the use of the recovery CDs. Whilst it may be unlikely that you will need them during the life of your computer, in order to avoid complications in future it is far better to be able to reach for the recovery media.

When sourcing a new computer, consider your operating system requirements carefully. If you really do want the previous version of windows, then buy one that was designed for use with that version of windows. Unless you want to upgrade to the newer version of windows at a later date, there is no benefit to buying downgrade rights.

Understanding Licenses

All software on your computer has a license associated to it. And with that license comes a user end license agreement (UELA). The purpose of the agreement is to define how many copies you are permitted to use, where it can be used, and how long you can use it for. Examples of licensed software include Microsoft Windows, Microsoft Office and Sage Accounts, to name but a few.

There are several different types of licenses available but I will focus on the two most common, since this is what the majority of small businesses and home users use.

The first, and most common, is 'Original Equipment Manufacturer' (OEM), which simply means that the license is intended for use only on the original equipment it was first installed on.

OEM is one of the most convenient ways of purchasing a license, since it is invariably procured when purchasing a computer (a typical OEM product is Windows 7 Professional, or Windows 8).

When compared to other types, OEM is extremely cost-effective. However it does have its limitations. Once the license is installed and activated, it will be forever linked to that computer. If the original computer dies, the license dies with it. This is because it is non-transferrable. Attempts to activate the license on another computer will often lead to errors suggesting software piracy has occurred.

However, there are some extenuating circumstances where an OEM license may be re-used. For example, if the motherboard or hard drive is replaced on the original computer, the license can still be reactivated as long as the other components inside the computer are the originals. This protects computer owners from additional costs when the original device becomes faulty and needs to be repaired.

An OEM license is usually provided without packaging or an installation CD. However, a certificate of authenticity will usually be included - either in paper form or adhered to the side of your computer.

OEM licenses can be purchased separately, but only by system builders (ie. an assembler, refurbished, or a pre-installer of computer system software). Invariably, OEM licenses must be purchased with hardware so that it can be demonstrated that the license 'belongs' to one or more hardware components.

Retail is more expensive than OEM, but this version permits the license to be transferred to another computer in the event that the original equipment dies. The number of times this is permitted varies between products. So too does the number of computers the license can be installed on. The important thing is to understand what you are getting when compared to other license options.

Unlike OEM products, retail products are usually available off the shelf, and are sold with packaging. A CD is usually included along with a license key, certificate or sticker.

It is important to know that the features of the actual software provided with OEM and retail is identical - it is only the terms of the license agreement that difference.

Should you go OEM or retail? It's really up to you. If you agree to the license and limitations, it makes financial sense to save a bundle with the low-cost OEM solution. But remember, if you are to go this route, speak to your system builder or computer manufacturer and be sure to purchase all the software you need at the point of order.

Installation or Integration

I grew up in a house with four siblings, so even as a child it was not unreasonable for my parents to expect me to keep my bedroom tidy. One day, my mother inspected my room before agreeing to my request for some pocket money. After discovering my half-hearted attempt to restore order to my room, my mother said something that resonates with me to this very day. She said, "Sally. If a job is worth doing, it is worth doing well."

Many years later I can still see she was right - especially when it comes to the installation of computer equipment.

I frequently witness the aftermath of lazy workmanship - especially when it relates to the installation of equipment like servers, computers or even replacement broadband routers. Introducing new equipment to an existing setup requires more than just installation. Plugging in a replacement router and expecting it to work is simply not enough - new equipment needs to be fully integrated. Without integration, frankly you may just as well have ordered a cardboard box.

Unfortunately, the business owner or end user is unlikely to notice that full integration has not occurred until after the work has been done and the engineer departed. Sadly it can be days before the poor quality of deployment is realized - for example when an end user discovers that something that was previously working is no longer operational at all. Worse still, it might not ever be noticed at all, as was the case with one such business owner I met recently.

The Managing Director of a local business was recommended to me, ten years after his first server had been installed. His reason for calling was that his network was running incredibly slowly, and his users were experiencing issues with mailbox sharing. They had assumed the issues were because the server was old.

Following a site survey, I was able to confirm that the server had been experiencing intermittent hardware failure. This was, of course, no major surprise to anyone given the server's age. However, this wasn't all I discovered. I was astonished to find that the server had never been fully integrated - and only one of the many features that were available with this particular equipment had been activated at all.

Had several of these other services been enabled, the client could have avoided the ongoing support costs that the same installation engineer charged for maintaining the mailboxes manually. Instead, the server ran for ten years, without these features ever being utilized.

With the benefit of hindsight, the client recalled that the engineer had struggled with the setup but was unaware that this resulted in the failure to activate certain features. The limited knowledge of this engineer meant that none of their early requirements had been fulfilled. Sadly, because the client had never owned a server before, he was none the wiser and had no reason to challenge it.

Had it been set up correctly, this server and all of its features would have spared this client multiple ongoing issues - not to mention all the extra support this unqualified support team continued to charge when his original systems continued to fail. How can you tell if your equipment has been properly integrated?

Having a vision is key. If you anticipated more flexibility and features from your new equipment, chances are you are right. Do not be afraid to ask for a second opinion. Trust your instinct.

Virus Nightmare

With the common cold doing the rounds on a frequent basis, we can all expect to succumb to the occasional sniffle. Over the counter medication will help suppress uncomfortable symptoms but in the end we have to let it run its course whilst taking plenty of rest. Provided the symptoms are nothing more sinister, the issue will pretty much resolve itself.

A computer virus shares similarities with a biological virus - it needs a host with a weakened immune system to survive, and it can multiply rapidly in a very short space of time.

Unfortunately, the likelihood of a computer virus resolving itself is less likely. Anti-virus (AV) products are designed to detect the presence of a virus before it is unleashed, by neutralizing the malicious code behind it. However, if a virus is launched by the end user before the protection tool has neutralized it, it can become a game of cat and mouse between the virus itself and the anti-virus software that is rapidly trying to eliminate it. At this point, you are likely to require a more hands-on approach, which increases the potential for increased IT support costs.

It should be remembered that anti-virus software is merely prevention - it is not the cure. The presence of the AV protection should not mean the end user can throw all caution to the wind with blatant disregard for the consequences - each must accept responsibility to safeguard against viruses at all costs.

Computers with no anti-virus protection, or expired anti-virus protection, are like a weakened immune system. Combine this with a click-happy individual and you might be asking for trouble.

A computer virus will wreak havoc on the operation of a computer. Some malicious software may reside undetected, silently gathering information and intercepting financial details from the unsuspecting user; others might display a message on a specific pre-determined trigger date then immediately unleash an aggressive attack by encrypting data before asking for a ransom of financial reward in exchange for the key to decrypt these now inaccessible files.

Exactly how these viruses are able to hijack your computer varies massively. For example, the virus known as "Trojan Horse" disguises itself as an attachment to an email, or a web browser file download. Once in your system, they allow in other malicious intruders - compromising the security of your system, not to mention your personal privacy. The 'worm' is a type of virus that takes advantage of security flaws in your computer – enabling it to multiply over your network (this is a nightmare if you operate a computer that is part of a shared network of other computers).

Whatever the objective of the particular strain of computer virus, the best defense on a Windows computer is to ensure the following housekeeping:

- avoid opening email attachments from unknown senders
- ensure windows updates are run regularly
- protect your computer by inoculating it with anti-virus software and be sure it is kept up to date.

There are many anti-virus software solutions available for sale, and some are more effective at protecting and neutralizing viruses than others. No matter what anti-virus software you invest in, it is crucial that you keep it up to date at all times. Every product is different, but they will all have the feature that allows you to both automatically and manually control these updates, so be sure to familiarize yourself with how this is done.

Combine the recommended housekeeping methods with user vigilance, and you will find your exposure to viruses and other malicious software is greatly reduced.

Desirable Domains

There is a lot of benefit to owning a domain name – whether it is for your business or personal use. A domain name is simply a unique string of letters that you can use to create an email or a website address. An example of a domain name is bloodycomputerbooks.com.

Without the technical know-how you could be forgiven for thinking that setting up a domain name requires technical skill. I have set up literally dozens of domains, for business and home use. The process is the same for both, and it is easier than you think.

A domain name is an asset, so it is important that it is registered correctly in order to ensure you never lose control of that asset. Registering a domain name yourself does not mean you must be the one to design a website for it - you may still need help for this part. Most web designers will happily design a website and publish it to a domain they did not reserve themselves. By retaining control of the domain registration process, even if you end up parting with your web designer, you don't part company with your asset.

It is important to understand that the World Wide Web is actually based on a string of numbers, called IP addresses. However, for anyone wanting to look at a website, no one would ever remember a string of numbers so, instead, domain names are used to translate those numbers - thereby taking the internet user to the correct address on the web.

Owning a domain name is like owning a phone number – once purchased, it remains yours until such time as you stop paying for it.

Domain names must be registered through an internet service provider (ISP). There are many ISPs to choose from, but I like to stick to the UK based ISPs.

To register a domain name, you must start by going to your chosen ISP's website. The option to purchase a domain name is likely to be the first option on the screen. The ISP will prompt you with a few questions, including your choice of domain name. If that domain name is already taken, it will prompt you for another. The whole process should take no more than 10 minutes to complete and you will be asked for credit card details to pay for your purchase.

With the purchase of each domain you will get your domain name and 12 months domain name hosting (you can select 2 year registration or more if you wish). Domain name hosting is NOT the same as website and email hosting – these are additional services that you need to add later. They cost extra, so don't bother adding them until you need them.

Once your domain is set up on your internet service provider's website, you will notice that your domain name can be managed by way of a user control panel, provided by your chosen internet service provider. Accessing your domain's control panel is possible only with valid login credentials - you will be asked to create these when you first register the domain, so be sure to write them down and store them safely so that you can access your control panel later.

Now you have your domain name in your control panel, you have full control of any related charges associated to that domain.

You may, of course, want to appoint a web site designer, who is likely to charge a fee for the design service. However, they should not need to add extra charges for hosting, since you will be able to add the hosting service yourself within your control panel. All you need to do is ask them what kind of hosting they need and you then pay for it within your control panel. Your internet service provider will help you, and it will avoid you incurring the cost of the web designer's hosting fees.

You may need help making changes in the control panel, but maintaining ownership of the domain name means you will never lose control of your asset.

For more information on domain management, visit www.bloodycomputersbook.com/resources

Chapter 10
Best Practice

Plan ahead

IT issues are like buses - either they don't show up for ages, or several arrive at the same time. Even with best endeavors, there is no way of escaping IT issues, but when and how should you escalate them to your third-party support?

When a plasterer quotes you for a job he is likely to offer you a better deal if you have multi-rooms done at the same time. This is because he will be taking into account the time needed for initial setup, so it is in your best interest to utilise his time wisely. IT support is similar. In order to provide you with IT support, your consultant will need to schedule in the appropriate time to complete the work. If a site visit is required, often a minimum one hour callout will be imposed. Even remote support is likely to carry a minimum charge.

Assuming your support charges are levied in accordance with the actual time spent, it is in your best interest to facilitate effective use of the time tech support spends assisting you.

Of course, if the IT issue is critical you will probably want to escalate the case right away and request priority response.

But for non-critical issues, a really useful cost-saving technique is to compile a list of IT support issues first, and then present them to tech support in one go. Consolidating your list will allow the consultant to be much more proactive in their approach.

If a list is provided ahead of the visit, the consultant can categorize support based on where they need to be in order to deploy a fix. For example, if several of the IT issues require some post-configuration on the server, the consultant can manage these all at the same time. It might even require some attention a day or so before the visit, in which case the consultant will have the means and opportunity to be more organized - getting some of the prep work done before the site visit.

Some of the most productive site visits I have ever attended have been those where my client has provided me with a list ahead of my appointment. As a support specialist, I find that some things are much easier and quicker to handle remotely - allowing me to spare my client from excessive time on site.

In the past, I have been invited to address IT support issues by way of an open day - that is where I am not provided with a list of issues beforehand, but just simply arrive on site with a view to spending the day addressing anything and everything that everyone can think of. This would require a visit to each of the individual users, reviewing their issues and assisting on the spot.

Whilst this can be effective approach, this method does impact upon the transparency of the work being completed; there is also an increased risk of duplication, or worse still, excessive to-and-fro on the part of the consultant. Additionally, the reporting process is compromised because many of the issues will be resolved but not documented.

There are other benefits to planning ahead too. It enables the consultant to prepare any supporting literature which may benefit end users, as well as provide an approximate duration of the anticipated time and confirm any related costs.

Consider appointing your nominated in-house systems administrator the task of consolidating the list and emailing it over to tech support ahead of their visit. This person may already know how to resolve some of the items on this list, thus reducing IT support costs further.

> For a sample support enquiry form, visit
> www.bloodycomputersbook.com/samples

Asset Bag

Many of us enjoy the task of unboxing new equipment. But in our endeavors to reveal the sleek new laptop or high-spec computer inside, we rarely pause to ask ourselves the importance of the rest of the contents of the box, let alone consider retaining the receipt.

Whenever my IT support services company supplies IT equipment to our clients, such as a new computer, laptop or server, we do not just provide the end product - we provide an asset bag too.

An asset bag is used to secure and protect critical assets relating to the purchase (which might otherwise be discarded along with the packaging). The value of this asset bag should not be underestimated. Not only does the bag and its contents help to maintain the integrity of the history relating to that computer, it also helps to keep safe all of the extras the manufacturer wanted you to have.

When your new equipment arrives, the box is likely to contain one or more CDs. The fact that these CDs are rarely needed to get you operational on the first day can lead to the misguided assumption that they are irrelevant. On the contrary, they are an asset and should be retained regardless.

The contents of these CDs vary, but typically include recovery tools, drivers and other software applications pre-installed on your computer. In the event that your PC needs to be rebuilt, these CDs are likely to prove invaluable to the IT consultant. Without them additional time and charge could easily be incurred.

There are other items you should retain in your asset bag too:-

User Manuals: Even though you might never read it, the manual is also worth keeping. Not just as a useful point of reference, but because it will enhance the value of your equipment should you ever wish to resell. You only need to look on e-bay to know that second-hand equipment sold with the original user manual is usually pitched at a slighter higher price.

Purchase Invoice: The final all-important thing to store in the asset bag is a copy of the purchase invoice. Imagine several years from now, how useful it will be to quickly and accurately determine the date the computer was purchased, along with information relating to the exact make and model, and exactly where you bought it.

Creating an asset bag is effortless. Not only will it provide you with a product history, it has the potential to reduce the cost of ownership by protecting the associated assets.

If your equipment provider does not supply you with an asset bag, create one yourself (a plastic zip bag lends itself perfectly). An asset bag is not limited to just computer and server equipment either - consider having an asset bag for printers and other IT equipment too - even if it is just for the safe storage of the copy of the receipt and user manual.

Keep your asset bag safe and easily accessible, and you will be surprised how impressed tech support will be that you are able to furnish them with these frequently discarded items when they ask.

Service & mot

When a brand new computer is switched on for the very first time, it will be running at optimum performance. In its 'factory default' state, the PC or laptop is free from outdated software, unwanted programs and other resource-draining add-ons that impact upon computer speeds over time.

Adopting a vigilant approach to the use of your computer and performing regular windows updates will help extend your systems reliability. However, any computer that has access to the internet and is pre-loaded with application software will require a degree of maintenance in order to safeguard its security, stability and performance.

The objective of a computer service is to diagnose performance problems, identify and install software updates, perform system housekeeping and resolve any application errors. It is also an opportunity to review system health, and validate the status of backup.

In the same way your car benefits from a regular service by a qualified professional, so too does your computer, laptop or server. Whilst I advocate DIY, and encourage users to take on as much of their system maintenance and housekeeping as possible, the importance of servicing your devices properly cannot be underestimated.

There are several things you need to know in order to successfully and safely maintain your computer:-

Avoid free software: You have only to google-search the phrase "my computer is running slowly" to find a plethora of tools that claim to be able to address the lag in your operating system. While this all sounds promising there can be many unexpected drawbacks to free software of any kind, so it is wise to be skeptical and careful.

Free versions of any program are often a marketing tool, designed to allow you to sample the product before investing in the paid version. However, free software can also produce income through advertising, so during the installation process you might unwittingly install unwanted banner advertising, which at best is borderline malware.

If you do want to try out a product, ensure you download safe software that has been recommended by an authority or trustworthy site.

Virus updates: Virus and malware are one of the most common causes of slow and unresponsive systems. Ensuring your computer is up to date and scanned regularly will ensure that protection is maintained. Although most anti-virus products scan your system automatically and are monitoring activity live-time, it is best practice to open your anti-virus and malware tools frequently in order to manually check the date of the last update and to invoke an occasional scan.

Potentially Unwanted Programs (PUP): PUPs are sneaky add-ons which are often attached to free downloads. Web browsers are notoriously overwhelmed by PUPs - leading to poor surfing speeds and frustrating website redirects. In some cases, these programs can be removed by using the add/remove programs tool in your computer's control panel. However, malicious or bad tools might require more experienced attention to ensure their safe removal.

Combine user management and housekeeping with a regular bi-monthly or quarterly service from an experienced professional. Regular servicing will facilitate proactive checks - allowing any potential system failures to be quickly identified.

Disaster Recovery Plan

Protecting your company's investment in its technology infrastructure and ensuring your firm's ability to conduct business are the key reasons for implementing an IT disaster recovery plan (DRP).

A DRP is a documented set of procedures or processes intended to ensure the protection and recovery of your company's IT infrastructure in the event of a disaster. The disaster could be natural, environmental or man-made - such as fire, flooding or theft. It might also come about as a result of malicious intent, accidental damage or unexpected catastrophic system failure.

Whilst the effects of a disaster cannot always be avoided, it is possible for the impact to be minimized. In the event that all or part of the IT operation is rendered unusable, the primary objective of the DRP is to protect business continuity, and safeguard against data loss and downtime.

The first step to introducing a disaster recovery plan is to consider your single point(s) of vulnerability. This could include your server, PC's running specialist software - even printers and routers.

Years ago, one of my clients introduced a very effective DRP when he realized that the stability of one of his PCs was crucial to business continuity. This particular computer was running a bespoke 'clocking-system' which was written specifically for his company. Unfortunately, the designer of this software went into liquidation, eliminating all hope of any further product development. Consequently the clocking system was frozen, rendering it compatible with Windows 95 only (which was the current operating system at that time) with no scope for migration to future versions of Windows.

In order to protect his investment, he immediately purchased two additional Windows 95 computers, and had the original PC cloned to these two new PCs in order to gain two identical, ready-to-go spares for his business-critical PC. In short, these three PCs extended the life of the clocking system by fifteen years.

These days, computers and servers can be cloned or replicated. Identify your most mission-critical equipment and consider talking through your options with your IT consultant. If necessary, ask them to perform a risk assessment to help develop a disaster recovery plan - before it's too late.

Switchover

As a two car family, my husband and I enjoy the benefits of motor-vehicle switchover. That is, if his car breaks down he has the option to use my vehicle, and vice-versa!

In computer terms, switchover is a swap to a redundant or standby computer, server, or other hardware upon the failure or abnormal termination of an existing device. Switchover requires human intervention.

Failover is the same as switchover, only it is automatic and usually operates seamlessly, without warning.

Switchover and failover are ideal solutions in disaster recovery planning since both facilitate recovery in the event of a disaster.

The automated features of failover have many uses. One of the best applications for failover is with broadband services. Many companies rely on their broadband, but invariably have only one service provisioned. In the event that their existing broadband service drops, without failover, continuity and business process can be compromised. Failover in this instance would require two broadband services into the building. With the appropriate equipment, failover could occur seamlessly between the two service providers – in affording a high degree of reliability and uptime.

Automatic failover can also be configured for servers and other network equipment too; however, this usually requires specialist equipment and installation.

Switchover is highly attainable, because there are no limits to the number of devices you can have on standby (budget permitting). There are many mission-critical components on your network that lend themselves to easy swap-out, but there are several common devices that you might want to consider having spares of:

Computers can be easily cloned. That is, one PC copied to another. The benefit of cloning computers and keeping one in safe storage is that, in the event of the first PC suffering from failure, the pre-configured spare can be used in its place.

Broadband Routers. Many broadband providers issue free routers with their service, so consider asking your provider to send you a spare. In the event of a router failure, having this spare will eliminate any unnecessary downtime you might otherwise incur waiting for a replacement. It also acts as an excellent test device too - if your broadband is down and you suspect your router is faulty, the pre-configured spare will enable you to confirm your thoughts.

Printers. Many printers are seen as business-critical tools, based on their features. For example, high speed printing or colour outputs can render a printer hugely important to productivity. Having a backup like-for-like printer on standby will ensure zero disruption to your specialist printing demands.

Network switches. Switches make excellent spares, since most require no pre-configuration or setup. If your existing network switch fails, your entire network of computers will be affected. Consider having a spare like-for-like network switch, so that you do not have to wait for tech support to bring you a replacement.

Of course, you may need to ask your tech support team to configure computers, routers and printers before you set them aside as spares. It would also be prudent to ask for a demonstration on swapping over the device, then, testing the spare before boxing it away.

This will ensure your ability to independently swap the device over when the time comes to replace the original - without having to incur any delays scheduling a reactive visit from tech support.

Backup

I am sure that, if asked, most of my clients would confirm there is one thing I am particularly obsessive about - and that is data backup.

My attention to detail in this particular topic stems from the days when I was employed as an IT Manager for a garments manufacturer. It was during this time I discovered the absolutely critical need for backing up company data.

One of my many responsibilities was to co-ordinate and manage the server backups. We used a tape drive at the time, and each night before leaving I would remove the tape and take it with me in my handbag.

One Friday evening, as I was preparing to depart for two weeks annual leave, I ran the backup, then took the tape home with me as usual. Before leaving, I inserted the next tape in the sequence ready for the next week. However, the following Monday morning, as I was enjoying my first lie in, my boss called to say there had been a burglary at work over the weekend. All of the computer equipment had been stolen – including the server.

This was serious. The entire organization was not only without any tech, but all of this business's intellectual property was gone. My boss then asked me a question that resonates to this day:

"Sally, have you got a safe copy of the last backup?"

At that moment, I realized I had been performing the backup routine on autopilot, so I could not be 100% sure I had the tape without checking. The hurried dash to retrieve the tape seemed to occur in slow motion. When I finally located my bag I began rummaging through it rapidly – as if my entire life depended upon its whereabouts. As soon as I located the tape, I found myself embracing like it was a long lost child.

I exhaled a sigh of relief, before an awful doubting question dawned from within; "Did the backup to this tape complete successfully?"

The fact was, I could not recall whether or not I had checked the backup logs. Without a server to restore to, this question went unanswered for several hours, whilst everyone waited for the delivery of new equipment. Once it all arrived, the recovery operation began. It seemed like an age before I was able to attempt to restore from the backup. All eyes were on this single tape, which cost just £1.20 to buy and yet held the entire company's data worth over five million pounds to my employer. The device was mounted, the application started and the settings for recovery initiated. Then we had to wait.

Within just a few moments, we were relieved to see that the familiar directory structures were starting to reappear. Recovery was 100% successful – our adopted routine and the tape had saved the day. And the most valuable lesson was learned.

Data is the most important aspect of your IT infrastructure. The operating system and other software can be reinstalled but it may be difficult or impossible to recreate your original data.

Backup is a fundamental part of your disaster recovery plan. It is a copy of your company's intellectual property and a crucial prerequisite to recovering from system failure. Removing the backup from site is also critical in order to safeguard against potential disaster such as fire, flood or theft.

Ensure backup logs are reviewed daily. If the backup tool facilitates email reports, be sure this is enabled - if not you will need to check the logs manually.

Appoint at least two members of staff to monitor the backup. This will eliminate user error and will allow for staff absences. Ensure the backup media is being rotated and regularly removed from site.

Introducing a formal backup procedure as described above is a great ways of protecting yourself from data loss.

About the Author

Sally Latimer-Boyce lives in Northamptonshire, UK with her husband and son.

Sally is an established technology expert, with a proud reputation and proven track record of managing IT problems and supporting companies with their technology requirements. Sally is co-owner of Serendipit² (IT Services) Limited - a successful IT Consultancy based in Northamptonshire, which was incorporated in 2004.

Operating as an 'outsourced insider', Sally offers herself as a dedicated Account Manager to her loyal client base and is committed to providing continuity, building relations, and cutting costs. Her knowledge of technology is comprehensive and relevant, and she has transformed the IT infrastructure for many hundreds of businesses.

Personable and assertive, her strong communication skills allow her to interact with people from every walk of life. She is inspirational, self-motivated and tremendously passionate about sharing her knowledge to empower others.

"Bloody Computers" manifested itself from the authors own early experience of a computer failure. At a crucial moment, Sally's PC crashed irreversibly, triggering a loud outburst of the words "bloody computers!". This phrase resonates with many users to this day and as such, bloody computers is used frequently to help promote Sally's IT Consultancy business. It was also a fitting title for this book.

Made in the USA
Charleston, SC
09 September 2015

Printed in Great Britain
by Amazon

YOUR HEART

♡(♡)

MY HEART

we used to sign our love letters like this

This is for you. ♥

Bee-Side PLAYLIST

Maps by The Yeah Yeah Yeahs
Nineteen by Tegan and Sara
I'll Be Your Girl by The Decemberists
River by Leon Bridges
The Way I Do by Madeleine Kelson
Emily I'm Sorry by boygenius
All Hail the Heartbreaker by The Spill Canvas
Every Man Has a Molly by Say Anything
LGFUAD by Motion City Soundtrack
Hunger by Florence + The Machine
The Archer by Taylor Swift
Going To Georgia by The Mountain Goats
Fast Car by Tracy Chapman
Moon Song by Phoebe Bridgers
Writer In the Dark by Lorde
A Decade Under the Influence by Taking Back Sunday
I Wish You Would by Taylor Swift
Keep Me in the Open by Gang of Youths
Selected Poems by The Gaslight Anthem
Your Ex-Lover Is Dead by Stars
A Better Son/Daughter by Rilo Kiley
Go West (demo) by Austin Lucas
Silver Springs (Live from The Dance) by Fleetwood Mac
World Spins Madly On by The Weepies

These are ancient.

Aphrodite Made Me Do It 2019
Artist: Lauren Zaknoun

Artemis Made Me Do It 2022
Artist: Lauren Zaknoun

Persephone Made Me Do It 2023
Artist: Lauren Zaknoun

myth
& magick
series

(feminist, witchy explorations
of Greek mythology relating to
modern issues / out with
Central Avenue Publishing)

Small Ghost 2015 - Artist: Lauren Zaknoun

Instead of Writing our Breakup Poem 2016
Artist: Trista Mateer

Poetry is Undead 2018 - Artist: Trista Mateer

the chapbooks

(short, handmade collections)

When the Stars Wrote Back 2020
Artist: Jessica Cruickshank

When the Stars Wrote Back (2nd edition) 2022
Artist: Trista Mateer

girl, isolated 2021 – Artist: Trista Mateer

is it okay to say this? 2022 – Artist: Trista Mateer

The Dogs I Have Kissed 2015 - Artist: Krystle Alder

[Redacted] 2016 - Artist: Eric Scribner

Before the First Kiss 2016 – Artist: Amanda Oaks

dragonhearts 2019
Artist: Lauren Zaknoun/Trista Mateer

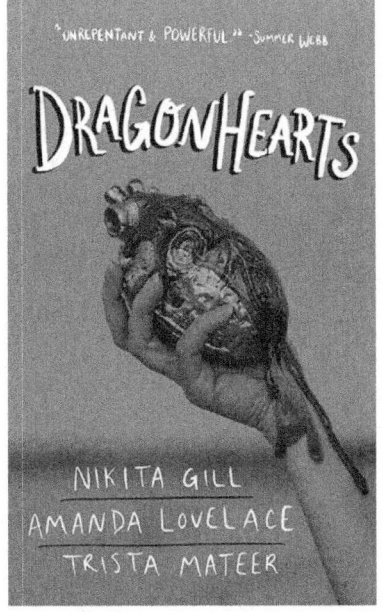

Honeybee 2014 - Artist: Krystle Alder

Honeybee 2018 - Artist: Marissa Johnson

Honeybee (hardcover) 2019
Artist: Marissa Johnson/Trista Mateer

Honeybee UK Edition 2020
Artist: Marissa Johnson and Hero Press

Poet's Corner

Moonie Ponds, Victoria, Australia

Where the second half of Honeybee was written and the bulk of the book was put together.

2013 - 2014

a little behind the scenes

National Poetry Month Prompts 2020

1. Make a blackout poem out of a recent news article.
2. Describe a childhood memory.
3. Write a poem from the POV of half of a fictional couple.
4. Write a dating profile as a poem.
5. Write a poem referencing a book.
6. Write about what you hope next March will be like.
7. Reference a social media platform by name.
8. Write a love letter to whatever is bringing you joy.
9. Pull three interesting words from your favorite song and use them in a poem.
10. Write a poem to "you." Don't disclose who the poem is to. Get something off your chest.
11. Write a poem that is a conversation between two people.
12. Be honest about what scares you.
13. Write a poem about something yellow.
14. Write a poem about or inspired by a specific city/place.
15. Use the phrase "the night we met" in your poem.
16. Write an argument for or against texting an ex.
17. Write a poem that mentions a specific kind of flower.
18. What does nostalgia mean to you?
19. Write about the last hard lesson life taught you.
20. What do you think about before you fall asleep at night?
21. Write a poem about a platonic relationship in your life.
22. Give yourself some kind of closure.
23. Use any variation of the phrase "I will never forgive you."
24. Write a poem about leaving.
25. Write a poem that takes place in a bedroom.
26. Write a piece that rhymes but don't expect perfection from it. Let it be whatever it comes out as.
27. Write a concrete poem/a shape poem. The visual appearance of the poem looks (at least a loosely) like the subject or theme of the poem. Like an apple-shaped poem about apples. Close enough even if it's just a little circular.
28. Write an "after" of This Is Just To Say (the plum poem) by William Carlos Williams. Could be a response, imitating the style, a poem disguised as a meme etc. Credit "after William Carlos Williams" under the title.
29. Write a poem mentioning breakfast food.
30. Freewrite. Fill at least half a page but only share one line.

National Poetry Month Prompts 2019

1. Write a letter to your younger self.
2. Acknowledge in the poem that you're writing a poem.
3. Use the word "golden" in your piece.
4. What does tenderness mean to you?
5. Describe a color without using the name.
6. What is poetry to you?
7. Write a poem from the perspective of a fictional character.
8. Make a list of reasons for staying alive.
9. Personify an emotion. Love. Anger. Sadness. Give it a physical form, actions, and a voice.
10. Write about a city you never want to see again.
11. Get back to basics. Love poem, ABCB rhyme scheme.
12. Base a poem on the last text you sent.
13. Make a blackout poem from the lyrics of a song.
14. Write a poem that mentions one of the following: lemons, apples, clementines, pears, blackberries.
15. Write a poem that includes two of the following: star, knight, fairy, queen, enchanted, cursed, fate, thieves.
16. Write a poem about cruelty.
17. Write a poem from the perspective of your ex.
18. Start your poem: "In the dream,"
19. Make a blackout poem from a Wikipedia article.
20. Write a series of newspaper headlines about your life.
21. Modernize a fairytale.
22. Write a response or a pt. 2 to a previous poem of yours.
23. Use the word "tomato" somewhere in your poem.
24. Google acrostic poems and try to write one. Don't take it too seriously.
25. Write a list of questions you have for someone. An ex. God. Your parents. Someone dead. Etc.
26. Pull a tarot card, look up the meaning, write about it. (You can use a free online tarot pull generator.)
27. Use water as imagery or a metaphor/simile.
28. Write about teeth or spit or longing.
29. Write about growing or bursting or blooming.
30. Free-write or journal about your month. Black everything out except the last line.

Unsolicited Tips On Writing Poetry

1. Experiment, don't be afraid to be a little weird, don't over-edit yourself. Many of my best pieces were written during the National Poetry Month challenge. Annually in April, poets attempt to write thirty poems in thirty days, usually posted to social media with hashtags like #NaPoMo or #NaPoWriMo. Even if you keep the poems to yourself, this is an excellent way to learn under pressure. The work that comes out of this month is often rushed and experimental. You don't have time to think too hard. You don't have time to edit your voice out of the poem. They sound like you. Taking part in this really helped me figure out my voice as a young writer and it still pushes me out of my comfort zone today.
2. If you're ever not sure what you're trying to say or what you want to write about, journaling is incredibly helpful. Observe the world, find it interesting. Even just keeping iPhone notes about your day or weird conversations you overheard or words you like—it helps flesh out your view of the world, it gives you an artistic foundation on which poetry can be built. You don't have to sit and wait for inspiration when you can just open your notes and pick something to turn into art.
3. Write what you need to write about. Even if it's just love poems. Find a way to be honest without giving away too much. Keep secrets. Keep things to yourself. Don't write about what you're not ready to share.
4. Read your poems out loud to edit them.
5. Read widely. Consume a broad range of media.
6. Accessibility is the key to being read. Make peace with that. If you are writing for only yourself, you don't have to worry about it but if you want community and if you want readers, you need to write in a way that speaks to them.
7. You don't have to put a book out or start a poetry account or submit to lit mags and journals to be a poet. You can just keep your closet notebook or write your little Notes app poems. Readers and accolades don't make you a poet. Writing poetry does. (Sounds obvious but people forget.)
8. You don't have to write every day but I try to do something that flexes my creative muscles every day.

About the Author

~~Trista Mateer is a Tumblr poet~~   ~~Instagram poet~~   ~~TikTok poet~~   ~~[????]~~   ~~best known for being sad and sapphic online.~~   ~~This is her first~~ ~~fifth~~   ~~tenth collection of poetry~~

Trista Mateer is the award-winning, bestselling author of multiple poetry collections including the mythology-inspired *Aphrodite Made Me Do It* and sapphic cult-favorite *Honeybee*. She writes about love and everything else. Her work has appeared everywhere across the internet over the last decade.

@tristamateer on tiktok, tumblr, instagram, etc.
tristamateerpoetry.com

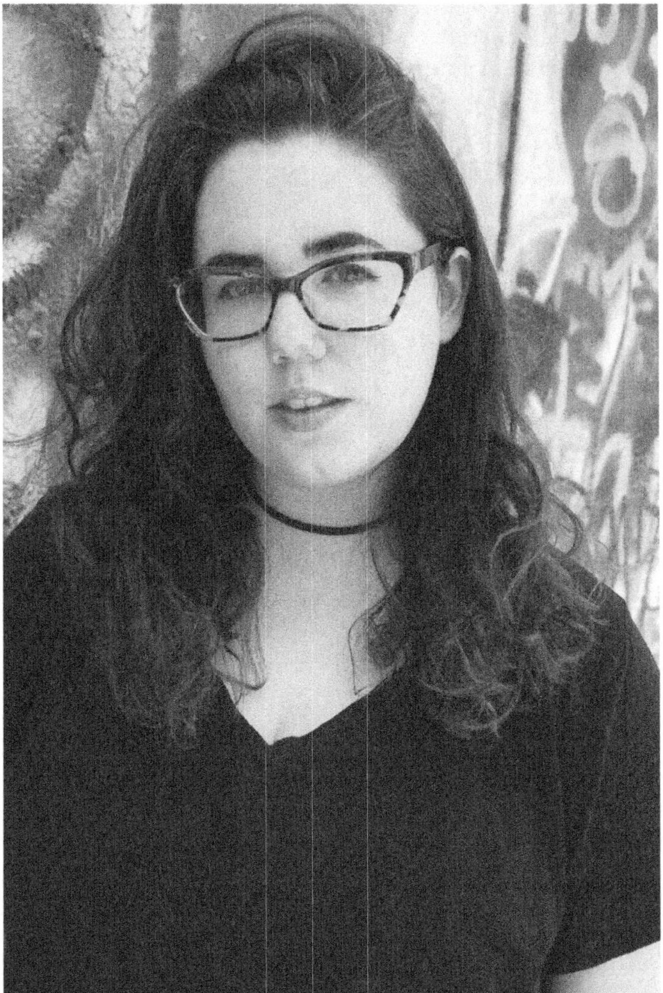

Recommended Reading

If Not, Winter: Fragments of Sappho by Anne Carson & Sappho
Mouthful of Forevers by Clementine von Radics
The Surrender Theory by Caitlin Conlon
Viraha by Yena Sharma Purmasir
Crush by Richard Siken
Paper Girl and the Knives that Made Her by Ari B. Cofer
We Were Young by Fortesa Latifi
Crybaby by Caitlyn Siehl
These Are the Words by Nikita Gill
The Universe of Us by Lang Leav
Pangaea by Hinnah Mian
Shelter by Kevin T. Norman
Instinct to Ruin by L Mathis
This Is All I Have To Give You by Clara McGowan
Itch by Zane Frederick
When You Ask Me Where I'm Going by Jasmin Kaur
Beast at Every Threshold by Natalie Wee
Teaching My Mother How to Give Birth by Warsan Shire
The Madness Vase by Andrea Gibson
Devotions by Mary Oliver
This Is The Journey by Alison Malee
Boatman by Ashe Vernon
Chokecherry by Lyd Havens
If My Body Could Speak by Blythe Baird
bone by Yrsa Daley-Ward
There Is Room for All of You Here by Michaela Angemeer
She Is The Poem by June Bates

On the craft of poetry & writing, try: *A Poetry Handbook* by Mary Oliver and *Bird by Bird* by Anne Lamott

Notes

You may have seen other versions of these poems online. Different line breaks, longer, shorter, different edits, etc. They're not incorrect versions, they're just young. All my rough drafts end up online and I make peace with them later.

Many of these pieces have been floating around the web uncredited for years but they can all still be traced back to my accounts on various platforms.

[Redacted], *Before the First Kiss*, *Instead of Writing Our Breakup Poem*, *Poetry is Undead*, and *dragonhearts* are out of print! *Small Ghost* is no longer available as a physical handmade chapbook, but it's on Kindle.

The *scrapped fairy-tale project* is still scrapped and Thistle Witch never metabolized into anything finished so excerpts are all that exist currently.

Poems credited only to *Honeybee* 1st edition do not appear in the second edition. The first edition is out of print. The book had a huge overhaul between its original self-published release in 2014 and its rerelease in 2018 with Central Avenue Publishing.

2018 Highlands, NJ – Photo by Caitlyn Siehl

2017 San Francisco, CA – Photo by Ari Eastman

2018 Toronto, Canada – Photo by Caitlin Conlon

Random House Children's, Sara Sargent, Words Dance, Amanda Oaks, Where Are You Press, Eunoia Review, Rising Phoenix Review / for supporting my work in many different ways.

Booksellers and librarians have my heart and gratitude.

Krystle Alder for designing my very first book covers. Lauren Zaknoun for her amazing work on the Myth & Magick covers. (and *Small Ghost!*)

Arch Budzar for creating the lovely paperback cover for this collection. Caitlin Conlon and Natalie Noland for their insightful edits. Exceptional, as always.

My wonderful readers for their constant support, their encouragement, their criticisms, their love letters, their rambling emails and DMs about heartbreak that they think I don't read. I would be nowhere without you. Some of you have been here from the very beginning and I can never thank you enough for that kind of support. I owe you more than I can say.

Caitlyn & Nikita for so much. Too much. Everything.

& so many others. I have been absolutely blessed to connect with some of the most amazing people doing this work over the last decade. Thank you endlessly.

Acknowledgements

With immeasurable thanks to:

THE POETS <3
Caitlyn Siehl, Nikita Gill, Caitlin Conlon, Natalie Wee, Clementine von Radics, Ari Eastman, Fortesa Latifi, Kristina Haynes, Lora Mathis, Lyd Havens, Yena Sharma Purmasir, Amanda Lovelace, Parker Lee, Ari B. Cofer, Iain S. Thomas, Michaela Angemeer, Alison Malee, Jones Howell, Madisen Kuhn, K.Y. Robinson, Shelby Leigh, Clara McGowan, Zane Frederick, Catarine Hancock, Caroline Kaufman, Ashe Vernon, Meggie Royer, Azra Tabassum, Jasmin Kaur, Blythe Baird, Heidi Wong, Schuyler Peck, Jade Mitchell, and more of course, always more. Poetry, as much as it is a singular anything, is a collective art. The community has changed a lot over the years. I still don't know where any of us would be without it.

Tumblr. Everyone has to start somewhere and if we're being honest I posted my first poems on Neopets.com a thousand years ago but Tumblr gave me an audience.

Assorted Muses for breaking my heart so spectacularly that I had to pick up a pen to heal it.

Michelle Halket, Central Avenue, Penny Moore, Jessica Pierce, Molly Ringle, IPG, Summer Webb, the team at

2016 Brooklyn, NY – Women of the World Poetry Slam
Caitlyn Siehl, Yena Sharma Purmasir, Audrey Hosford, Trista Mateer
Photos by Caitlyn Siehl

Thank you for being here.
Thank you for your support.

If you enjoyed this collection, please consider sharing this book with a friend.

And I deeply appreciate when you take the time to rate or review! Feels small but it helps me a lot and I always love to hear from you.

Thank you for reading, always.

♡ Trista

Fragments #34

In your anger and your despair
and your glorious, glorious youth
do not discount the idea of soulmates.

Discount the idea of a singular soulmate.

You still have way too much to learn
to be taught by one person.

Another love poem?
        Yes, another love poem. And another after that

God willing

I needed something to believe in
and it couldn't be me this time

so it's love   of course it's love

always has been

Come on bitch it's time to go.

We're backing away from the edge again.

We're going home   no not that one   yes that one.

The old one
the one that lives inside of you.

      Home as you remember it before you
understood it   home when it was golden.

Come on bitch the light is fading.

We're starting over
back at the beginning.

Nothing bad has happened to you yet
& Everything is made new again.

2023

Coffee Grounds & Orange Peels

I am making compost
out of our old love: piling up
all this hurt,
and hoping one day
something good can grow from it.

Tumblr, 2015

Once More, for Old Times' Sake

It's your voice I hear in the spaces between words.
I see the echoes of you in all of my poetry.
People do have roots. Think of our hands intertwined.
I was wrong. There's no harm in admitting it now.

> If there really is a universe parallel to this one,
> maybe we're brave there / maybe we're married
> / maybe it's sunny / and everyone we love /
> is alive.
>
> If there really is a universe parallel to this one,
> I don't want to know a damn thing about it.
>
> Schrödinger's happy ending.
> There's still a possibility it's there
> as long as I don't look at it / directly.

2023

God says I'm unrecognizable now, but I was made in her image.

                  How could I abandon this religion?
                  She made me a believer.

2023 – cut from *Persephone Made Me Do It*

Love is the only thing worth talking about
or writing down
or living for.

It was hell and I loved every minute of it.
It killed me and I'd do it again.
I plan to.

2020 – cut from *girl, isolated*

Trista Mateer · *I Swear Somewhere This Works*

~~Love never gets to be the biggest part of my story again.~~

Instagram, 2017

Afterthoughts

Online, I see web weaves of our love poems.
It's strange   being forced to look back on life
as I have written it.   Being inescapable.

Our love letters will outlive us. You were right.
We will be remembered.

      And I'll keep your books on my shelves and
only dust them off every five years or so
but I understand if mine are in a pit   out back.

This is what we signed up for. This is what we bled for.

There you are again. Funny running into you like that.
Just like I remember you. Just like I remember us.

Have you ever burned your tongue on a memory?

        This is exactly how we wrote it.
          I said I'd be missing you forever.

I don't ever think of you   except   when I do.

2023

And the Interviewer Asks:
Does Your Past Work Embarrass You? Do You Ever Look Back and Cringe?

I try not to blame my old self
for existing   so loudly

      and anyway   I'm the one still here
      speaking to the dead

      writing revisionist history

2023

Fragments #33

I'm looking back   I'm looking back

    I'm not looking back   I'm looking at you

You have to admit there's some kind of price you pay for learning you can sell your secrets online at nineteen.

(I regret nothing. I will not make amends.)

Someone tell me it was brave to do this.

Make it fine in retrospect.
Make it good.

All that suffering.   All that yearning.

Oh, weren't we in love?
And wasn't it good?
Wasn't it worth writing down?

*(Depends on how you remember it.
Depends on how you write it down.)*

2018–2023

Honey, I'm begging.
I'm down in the dirt for you.
Let's make it work. Just this once.

I know, I know.
I said it could happen
in another life
but   I want it here.

& I won't accept less.

Love lives or dies with you and me
right now.

TikTok, 2021

hearts can't live on hope alone, but

    god   *if they could*

TikTok, 2021

Fragments #32

I've been reading the old poems.   I can't believe you really put your name on all that. I can't believe I did.

Remember the bad champagne in the back room of that reading?   / a hand squeezing mine promising to keep in touch / *I don't know when I'm going to see you again but I'm going to see you again*

      Remember meeting at the airport? Remember leaning on my shoulder? Remember treating Siken like it was gospel   and not always wanting to die?

      I miss your handwriting. I miss your laughter. I miss our conversations   all the poetry we made out of regular living.

      driving across   New Mexico, the sunset over the mountains / Playing spin the bottle, playing guess the muse

      here's to the kiss and tell,
      here's to the stories you keep to yourself

I was lucky to skin my heart so hard on your pavement. I'm ready to get up and try again. Come with me. Let's see how fast we can go.

2013–2023

> (Soft reminder that I'm thankful for you every day.)
>
> Delivered

Loud Reminder that I would hang the Fucking Stars for you

I love you so much

Anonymous asked:

Trista, I'm so glad you exist.

I'm glad you exist too.

---

7. How has being a poet shaped your everyday experiences? Would you say your experiences differ from others since you look at everything through a poet's eye?

   I don't think my experiences are really all that different from anyone else's. I'm just taking better notes and making worse decisions.

Star Emoji
After "Heart Emoji" by Lyd Havens
A poem crafted out of texts I've sent to my friends.

HI I LOVE YOU / I didn't see you yesterday so my heart is screaming / but / it's always / screaming about something / I woke up from a dream about you / I just woke up from a dream about running through a grocery store with you, trying to find duck sauce / I had a dream that I was on a train and you were running to the station with your shoes in your hands / you're a big part of the / magic / in my life / I'm so proud of you / I am literally always wishing the best for you / you could read a grocery list and I'd call it a poem / queen of my heart / yes / star of my heart / yes / light of my life / yes / you own a fucking sword, I don't expect you to be this tender / I'm going to have to stop calling it lowkey / everything I feel is so loud / I have more to say than poetry allows sometimes / but / I'm so happy you're happy / there are words / at least / for that

dragonhearts, 2019

I will be tagged in our love poems
until I die and probably after.
I've made peace with that.
Even before I started writing,
I saw you everywhere.

2023

When I say I love you,
I mean:

I can't guarantee that everything
is going to be good and joyous
and okay forever
but

everything
is going to be good and joyous
and okay forever.

Instagram, 2020

Trista Mateer · *I Swear Somewhere This Works*

I might regret this in a few years
but it felt good to fall back in love with you

like a hand into last winter's glove

still warm
and familiar.

Instagram, 2020

Yeah, I'm here
again.
Foolish, I guess
but that's not new.
And you   are my oldest friend.
And one time you called me a peach
and then I wrote it
into all of my poems
        like a callback
           or a crumb trail.

My overused metaphor.
My overripe want.

I don't know.
I loved you for eleven years
and I never was sorry for it.

I'm still not.

Instagram, 2020
girl isolated, 2021

Fragments #31

I can't go another day choking back *I love you*
I feel it in my shoulders when I breathe

I love you
I love you   which really means I forgive you
which really means it's time for you to come home

what are you waiting for

2015–2023

Unspeakable Times

And still,
all I do is talk about her hands and her mouth
        so we're both damned.

No peace for magnificent sinners.

What good are prayers if God has cast me from paradise
for seeing stars in her eyes?

If God exists, he can meet me outside.
        This is what lovers do. We sing fight songs.

        We remade heaven on earth
                and I'll defend it with my teeth.

Go on, condemn me to hell.
The fire is already in me.
She put it there.

2023

MORE LOVE POEMS
MORE SOFT MOUTHS
MORE IMPULSIVE TATTOOS
MORE EMBARRASSING TEXTS
MORE SPILLING YR GUTS
MORE KISSING YR FRIENDS
MORE OPEN HANDS
MORE EMPATHY
MORE UNFLINCHING
EMOTIONAL HONESTY

Tumblr, 2016

love is a museum and
we fuck in it

Since you left.
I've met two
people with your
name.

It still hits me
in the gut every
time I have to
say it.

I missed you. Does it make me weak to say it?

Sometimes I forget we're not friends anymore.

I wake up with things to tell you.

or spent an hour on public transit just to get to your front door.

This is the closest I have been to you in four months

Top to bottom: 2013–2014, 2014–2015, and 2017
Poetry notes

Trista Mateer · *I Swear Somewhere This Works*

I'm so sick of reducing lovers to lessons:

How to let go.
How to stay.
How to ask for what the heart wants.

How to leave.

How to recognize disaster.

How to survive.

How to love.

Tumblr, 2016
[Redacted], 2016
When the Stars Wrote Back, 2020

Fragments #30

I'm still happy I met you
I'm still glad that it happened

       buttercups in my hair, your hair in my shower,
your hand on my throat, my knife in your back

You're leading me up the stairs to your apartment
       Do you remember that first night?

You're leading me up the stairs to your apartment

       My heart is making fists in my throat. My heart
is working overtime. My heart wants to use you as a
punching bag. My heart wants to bleed all over you

  tie you up on the tracks and watch the train come

but you   just want to hold   my hand

We could have left it right there.
I could have had it easy but I wanted it to be hard.
       I wanted the unpragmatic love story. I wanted
to run across the world for someone. I wanted

       I think I want too much.

It could be easy, you know.
Not with us, but with other people.

2015–2023

Trista Mateer · *I Swear Somewhere This Works*

I crawled
on broken glass
to get here.
You better believe
I'm living it up.
I will swallow stars
if I want to.
May my dreams come true.
May my enemies eat shit.
Times are tough
but I'm a fucking nightmare.
I have my boot
on the throat of hell
right now.
Watch me beat my demons
into submission.
Surviving's ugly work
and here I am,
so hideously alive.

girl isolated, 2021

Fragment #29

You'd think time would make me forget but everything is written down.

Remember?
Remember?
Of course I remember.

There is no forgetting.

2019–2023

Small Ghost Looks to the Future

thinks about flowers on her kitchen table and the way
light looks slipping through the blinds at 10am

thinks about the taste of strawberries
and other people's mouths fresh with toothpaste

thinks about airports and train stations and
how rain makes everybody feel a different way

thinks about bookshelves and frost and
instrumental movie soundtracks

thinks about how sweet it might feel to be soft again

thinks about thawing like ice

thinks about budding like spring

thinks about laughing until it doesn't hurt to breathe
anymore

thinks about how hard it is
to admit that she wants things
because it means she might not get them

                then she wants things anyway

Small Ghost, 2015

For Myself, When I Want to Die

There are trees still,
and you love those.
The smell of dirt and pine.
Sunshine on bare skin
almost feels like being touched
if you close your eyes.
The cat sleeps on your chest
to hear the sound of your heartbeat
and she'd miss that.
One day when your brain is calmer
you might be able to read books again.
There are people who love you
even if they don't really know you.
That doesn't always have to be a burden
or a wound.
It still feels good to write poems
if you don't show them to anyone.
It will not always be like this.
You don't have to believe that
but you have to believe something.

girl isolated, 2021

Yes it's true, the horrible things remain horrible
and even your mother won't always agree with you
and the weather is so heavy
all it does is remind you that you're not being touched.

I agree, the news is too ugly to watch today
and yes I know people have been cruel without reason
and your heart is hurting still
from things you won't tell your friends about.

I know.
I know.

I know it doesn't make it better that I know.
It is one thing to be seen
and another thing entirely to be held.

girl isolated, 2021

I hope one day
somebody loves you
so much

that they see violets
in the bags under your eyes,
sunsets in the downward arch
of your lips

that they recognize you
as something green,
something fresh and still growing
even if sometimes
you are growing sideways.

>   I hope one day
>   somebody loves you
>   so much
>
>   that they do not waste their time
>   trying to fix you.

Tumblr, 2013
Honeybee 2nd edition, 2018

Trista Mateer · *I Swear Somewhere This Works*

Poet,
on some level
you are a lonely person.

I mean, don't you have anyone else
to say all this shit to?

Instagram, 2022

Fragments #28

If we both look at the same moon and you still don't want to call to say goodnight then maybe we're not looking at the same moon anymore.

I'm sick in love.   I'm a bitch in hell.

We're staring at the same moon but I don't remember what you taste like and you don't have my number in your phone anymore.

All the wrong things are changing.

> And I'm stuck in the past
> the way all lovers get stuck in the past.
> > And I'm hurting
> > the way all lovers end up hurting.

I tell everyone who asks about you that we outgrew each other. I still don't know if that's the truth. Maybe we just got tired.

Maybe the moon has nothing to do with it.
Maybe you're not the same person.
> Maybe I'm not.

2014–2023

Fragments #27

I don't want to know how you are but
        I always hope things worked out for you.

I hope you're happy.   I hope you're okay.
I hope you never think about me.

Here's to you and the rest of your life. I want you

to have everything,

        absolutely everything.

2014–2023

kissing the wrong person goodnight.

Snapchat, 2014

I know a thing or two about

Snapchat, 2014

Fragments #26

Nothing I write is for you.
Everything I write is for you.
        Dealer's choice.

        The poems aren't about anyone specific.
I'm just talking to the moon.

(*You are the moon.*) (*You are not the moon.*)

I'm here
again
despite our worst intentions.

I never loved you.

I never loved anyone else like I loved you.

2014–2023

Lord what will become of my brand when I die

and was all of this for nothing

the years I unbecame myself
and grew palatable

the commodification

the performance work
of my sadness

you can train the bite away
but the ache for it lingers

I have forgotten so many things
I have forgiven so many things
all in the name of art

not even in my own name

Instagram, 2021

⟨ All iCloud

December 25, 2019 at 8:34 AM

the love poems I wrote for you

all of a sudden, fiction

November 7, 2020 at 8:17 PM

I am thinking of you, always.

⟨ All iCloud

August 16, 2020 at 4:08 AM

The worst part about forever
is that it means different things
to different people.

Cherry-Picking

I'm sorry for what I said
and for what I didn't say.
It could have gone better in the end
but there were good times too, I think.
In the middle and near the beginning.
Sorry for fighting dirty.
Sorry for being a fool.
Not all love is worth eulogizing
but here I always am, laying it to rest.
I still think of you
even when I say I don't.

2023

Fragments #25

[You're sitting on the edge of the bed eating your own heart like an apple and it never once occurred to you to stop.]

I repeat all of my mother's mistakes.
    I heard that love just takes and it takes.

    I'm lonely in the most untouchable way.

The room is spinning,   I'm spiraling again.

Unraveling
like a ball of yarn rolling across the living room floor

        right in front of everyone.

All our idols turned out to be sad and bitter people.

THERE'S STILL HOPE FOR ME THOUGH.

2020–2023

I want to be free of love so I stab it in my kitchen.
I push it from the top of the stairs.
I hide pieces of it under the floorboards.

I want to be free of love so I dig its blood
out from under my nails. I put arsenic
in its coffee. I smother it with my pillow
while it lies next to me in bed.

I dismember love. I grind love up
and feed it to strangers. I put love in a little box
in my attic and just go stare at it sometimes.

I want to be free of love
but then I look around

and love is excruciatingly everywhere.

2022

Release me
from the burden
of longing.

Instagram, 2019

Coming Home

It took me too long
to realize it was

not

romantic(, tender, or healthy)

to love someone else
more than I loved

myself.

Honeybee 1st edition, 2014
Honeybee 2nd edition, 2018

Trista Mateer · *I Swear Somewhere This Works*

You with the moon in your hand
You on the shore   You as the shore
And I'm waving goodbye but I don't remember
why I'm leaving / I never do

Instagram, 2023

Come kiss me
and numb the pain
of time passing.

2023

Time changes everything
and nothing

It's All So Light

Nobody is in love with me
and everything is still warm.
Still soft.
Still rosewater and a typewriter ribbon.
Still cookbooks and salt air and sheer black lingerie.
Still red lipstick.
Still mostly kind.
Still often uncomplicated.
Still mints at the bottom of my purse,
hair held back,
pulse thumping through skin.
Still sweet tea in a pitcher on the kitchen counter,
a cold glass with three lemon slices,
a full ice-cube tray.

Tumblr, 2016

And the Interviewer Asks:
What Is Poetry to You?
Can You Define It for Us?

No   but I can draw you a map

There is an intersection between Fiction
& Honesty

Poetry usually hangs out there,
yelling at passersby

2023

And the Interviewer Asks:
After All This Time, Why Do You Still Write?

      I don't know

I write to be understood
      I don't want to be understood

I write to be seen
      I don't want to be seen

I write to be remembered
      Maybe

I write out of spite
      Mostly

2023

The Poem Does Not Have to Be Good

The poem does not have to be good or noble or beautiful or succinct or long or terrifying or painful. The poem does not have to be kind or angry or about love or about trauma. The poem does not have to be a perfect 10 and it does not have to make strangers laugh or even cry. The poem does not have to resonate with anyone. The poem does not have to be personal or relatable or abstract or pretty. The poem does not have to be book-worthy or journal-worthy. The poem does not have to prove itself to anyone. It doesn't have to be a mirror or a window. It doesn't have to be a miracle.

It just has to say something
and then take a breath

and then find the courage to say something else.

When The Stars Wrote Back, 2020

I know I know
I have written so many similar poems

I have written so many different poems
    all screaming the same thing

        but I can't hear it

        so I keep writing

2023

Trista Mateer · *I Swear Somewhere This Works*

Everything is such a blur, looking back.

I slept with you just so you'd stop playing me songs on the guitar   offered my body up so you'd have something else to do with your hands.

Isn't that ugly? Isn't this predictable?
Sweeping the dust out from under the rug.
Arranging awful things to look like poetry.

The poem isn't really a poem.
The poem is an admission of shared guilt.
      Resentment, too.

The poem is an inability to leave the past in the past.
The poem doesn't mean anything other than:

Look,   *I'm still talking about things*
        that happened years ago.

        Even when it's about you, it's about me.

Reply to a song my ex wrote

2019 – cut from *When the Stars Wrote Back*

Accidentally Rambling

This poem is a few years late,
but I guess now is better than never.

I don't think closure is real.
Did I ever tell you that?

I don't know what's okay to say to you anymore.
Every line feels like a crossed one.

      How's your mother?

      Do you remember when I kissed you and I
meant it? Do you remember the times I didn't mean it?

We fought about all the wrong things.

Isn't it strange how easily trust can sneak out the door
if you don't watch it carefully? How it can slip
out of its collar and run down the street?

      I'm still asking questions
      you can't answer.

Do you think we deserved each other?
Have you finally mastered object permanence?
How hard is it to remember you have a girlfriend
when she's not in the same room as you?
Do you remember why I stayed when I found out?

      I don't.

Apple Pie Life

Now,

I want
what everyone always told me I would want.

Something quiet.
Something warm.
Something to get full on.

Instagram, 2019

I Think I Want Too Much

Love that crashes like potted plants
from fifth-story windows.

Love that bursts like an appendix.
Love that is consumed by itself.

Love that thinks only about the NOW NOW NOW.

Love like a floor-to-ceiling map of the world.
Love I keep sticking pushpins in.

Love that doesn't want to hold me back
from anything

but still won't let go.

Tumblr, 2015
When the Stars Wrote Back, 2020

Sometimes
love ends loudly.
Yowls like a sad beast in heat.
Gets blood all over everything.
Flings the door open
and makes sure everyone
can hear what's going on inside.

Sometimes
love ends quietly.
Packs its bags and
doesn't leave anything behind,
not even a button from a coat.
It says *I'm sorry*
and clicks the door shut behind it.
Takes a taxi to the airport
and sits in silence at the gate.

Instagram, 2020

When My Love Begs Me to Write a Happy Poem

I say okay.
Here it is.
Another poem about California.
Your mouth and the telephone.
All my weak spots.
How much I want to be
the scarf around your neck
in the winter.
How I forget what day it is
when you don't call.
How I let myself get so
wrapped up.
I say okay.
I don't know if this is a happy poem
but I wrote it for you.
That counts for something.

2019

Everyone I know
is wading closer back toward bad love.
        Bad love is a harsh phrase.
Sometimes it's just old love, stagnant love,
unwilling love, ugly love.

               Love that kicked you out last year—
               don't you remember it?

               Love that started house fires
               and then ignored all the smoke.

I say, *You don't have to burn like that anymore.*
And they say, *I know, I know, I know*,
but they still keep looking back.

Instagram, 2019

The world feels like it's ending,
of course I am calling you.
I barely hesitated at all.

I am calling because I love you.
I am calling because people are dying
and one day you could be one of them.

I am calling because I still have things to say.

    I never thought I'd have to call.

    Thought you'd be here already
    holding my hand
    and watching the smoke.

Instagram, 2020
girl isolated, 2021

Poem in Which I Ask the Moon Out (Again)

I know you said you needed space.
Tell me that you've had enough of it.
Tell me that you're sick of distance.
Baby, I am sick of distance.

Hello?

Sorry for calling again
it's just been such a strange year.
I miss everyone I've ever met
and you
most of all.

Are you there?

*The number you're trying to reach
has been disconnected.*

2020

I turned around in a crowd yesterday
because I thought I heard your voice.
This is what forgetting is like.

For a while everything sounds like you
and then nothing ever does again.

Instagram, 2018

Fine, I'll say it.
I had the dream about you
and the oranges again. I have written
the same poem at least four other times.
I miss the thought of you
in my bed. I can hold onto anything at night
if I want it enough
and I wanted it enough. I think
you wanted it too.
Inaction is the worst part
of everything.

I waited for you and I shouldn't have.
I still love you just the same.

Instagram, 2020

The thing about time
is the way it passes. It makes people sick.
Nostalgia   is the cure.
We sell our souls to things that remind us of home.

You remind me of home.   I wrote a poem once
where I said you didn't remind me of home   but
I wrote that ten years ago   and I'm a liar now.

Love makes you a liar sometimes.
We both know that's true.
         I have been in love   with you
for   a third   of my existence.

Fascinating.   And disgusting.

You could have paid for phone sex   instead of
ruining   my   life.

Instagram, 2020

Fragments #24

Bruised but still sweet
        a little too soft under pressure.

If I were a peach   you'd be the only person
I'd trust to get close to the pit of me.

        I'm talking about my heart.
        It's all I ever talk about /

I ate a peach today and it reminded me of you.
Got gin-drunk and it reminded me of you   too.

I figured out why you fell in love with me.
I remind you of something you grew out of.
Something young. Something naive.
All the bad parts of youth, but all the good parts too.
You know, like how I thought maybe I could
make a living off of writing poetry and how I thought

        LOVE WAS REAL AND WE WERE IN IT.

I keep trying to make the end of this poetic but
        you don't even have art on your walls.

        I'm talking about your heart.
        It's all I ever talk about /

When love ended   You pulled the pit out of me

2014–2023

Yes, I dreamt up a life with you
just so I could live inside of it.

                                          No, I don't have that dream
                                                                 anymore.

                                                                         LIAR

Instagram, 2019

Trista Mateer · *I Swear Somewhere This Works*

In the Sims 4 version of our lives,
I'm so busy kissing you
that I forget to put a roof over our heads.
We don't even paint the walls
until after we're married.
The dishes pile up
and we chase each other around them.

Tumblr, 2017

In the dream, we are strangers knee to knee on a train.
It's the most we ever touch.

        I still write about you.
I still end up here. There is something to be said for a
love that refuses to melt. A love stored in the freezer, in
a Ziplock bag. Stashed behind the ice cube tray. Always
willing to thaw, to forgive like spring, to pick up right
where it left off.

    You, cradling a phone in the crook of your arm.
    Me, crying about produce.

You call, and I answer. You say, *Do you know what an air
traffic control room looks like? All those switches and buttons
blinking? When I hear your voice, everything lights up all at
once for me. Nobody else does that.*

    I don't say anything eloquent.

So we're back on the train, with the knees,
only this time you're looking me in the face
and I'm staring out the window.

    What do you think happens
    when love gets left out too long?

Tumblr, 2017

Same Old, Same Old

Here we are again
at the base of this poem about a man
ashamed of the hands he touches other people with.
Too stubborn to admit love
when it's stuck in his throat like hard candy,
like juice gone down wrong.
He can't stop coughing it up.

Here we are again, me and this poem,
trying to persuade you that it's romantic,
not to be chased but to be held off,
to make friends with the waiting room
but not the people in it,
because the people keep changing
but me and this room
we just keep on
waiting.

Funny how things can tell you exactly what they are
and you'll still find a way to be surprised
and disappointed later.

It's not the room's fault that nobody likes waiting.
It's not the man's fault I keep crawling down his throat
and making myself a choking hazard.

Tumblr, 2017

Peaches

You've ruined peaches for me.

I can't eat one without thinking of your hands
dipping into my soft flesh, mouth dripping,
teeth skimming across skin, tongue lapping
at the excess:

greedy, greedy, greedy.

I am all rush and blush at a summer picnic lunch,
hands shaking at the farmers' market.

The Dogs I Have Kissed, 2015

Fragments #23

I hear your voice
and

even time surrenders.

        Everything stops for us.

I dreamt of your bed long after I stopped sleeping in it.
I still   pray at the church of your hands.

> *(She does not remind me of anything.*
> *Everything reminds me of her.)*

Everywhere I look,
I only see you.

2014–2023

Ask Again Later

I miss you so much it feels gross.
It feels wet. It feels nauseating.

I want to rip out my heart
and shake it like a magic eight ball.
*Is this okay, is this okay, is this okay
or does it make me weak?*

The Dogs I Have Kissed, 2015

Trista Mateer · *I Swear Somewhere This Works*

I see her everywhere, even in other people's love poems

It hasn't rained here in at least a month,
which means all the scrub brush
is the color of my ex-girlfriend's hair
and the dirt is always kicking itself up,
trying to land in somebody's open   mouth.

I cross the California state line for the first time in four
years and think: this is what it feels like to be a highway
in love with a parked car,   this is what it feels like
to sit on the doorstep of his house and not be let into it.

He is the highway
and the car
and the light in my attic
and the hand on the back of my neck.

       My unfinished love note. My locked door.

I had a dream
about being led into his home blindfolded.
He sat me on the bed and told me his father's name,
told me his favorite fruit, told me he loved me
but wouldn't look me in the eye.

What must it feel like to be so afraid of joy
that you won't let it walk across your living room
with the lights on?

2017

have you considered:
it might not be
the timing,
it might just be us

I DESERVE TO FEEL GOOD

MY LIFE IS NOT EMPTY

THINGS ARE GOING TO TURN AROUND

Fragments #22

Aphrodite Airs Her Grievances
Aphrodite Sings of War
Aphrodite writes a poem,
        doesn't remember who it's for

You   wanted a sacrifice and I made myself one.
I would have offered even if you didn't ask.
I am always trying to give myself up. I am always
trying to   find something worth bleeding for

      I miss   the stars and the ocean I crawled out of

I have chased the universe to its end   and run naked
through Eden   and I still can't fill this void

young hearts want to die for love, but
I just want to go home

2019–2023

Trista Mateer · *I Swear Somewhere This Works*

I still write poems for you
the same way other people
bring flowers to graves.

Tumblr, 2018
Artemis Made Me Do It, 2022

Fragments #21

Maybe I walked away from a good thing and let it define the rest of my life.

        [A woman alone, head over heart.]

I am insisting on the impossible.
I am still holding out hope.

I'm still carrying around sugar packets in my pockets,
      praying for rain.

And that won't change.
That's my character.
It's in my nature   to want   and to be sorry for it.

2017–2023

7 Lines for Adam

1. *Is that a mirror in your pocket? Because I see myself in your pants.* Or I used to, before you died.

2. *Excuse me, but I think you dropped something. My jaw!* And my sense of purpose, and my ideas about everything working out in the end. I'm sorry I couldn't go to the funeral. How was I supposed to stand over your casket when I still know what your mouth tastes like?

3. *I lost my phone number. Can I have yours?*
   And if I call, will you still answer?

4. *You know what would look great on you? Me.* Or that blue suit you wore to my grandfather's wake. You were wearing that suit the last time you asked me out to dinner. I've cried on that suit and so have you. I wonder if that's what they dressed you in.

5. *Did it hurt when you fell from heaven?*
   Can you do it again?

6. *Your legs must be tired because you've been running through my mind all night.* You've been keeping me up for a while now. What I want to know is, am I even allowed to carry this grief with me? Am I supposed to leave it somewhere? Am I supposed to know how to put it down?

7. I should have let you take me home.

Tumblr, 2017

Yes, I'll say it.

I wish love was a dream
I could wake up from.

I wish I didn't need
to be touched.

Instagram, 2020

"Closing Time" by Semisonic
Plays at Last Call

My heart is a bar and you tend to it.
Or you don't, but you might have if I let you.

> My heart is in a bar
> and you left yours there too, for a while.

Yesterday, I woke up to a world without you in it. I thought it was a joke but there was very little setup. Man walks into a bar, stays for eight years, dies in his sleep too young. I'm never going to get the punchline, but I keep trying.

Once, you made me throw up Fireball Whisky on my birthday. Once, you sobbed on my shoulder and I didn't tell you to move. Once, I wrote a poem about kissing you and wishing it was someone else. I don't have a working list of things I regret, but I think I'm going to.

My heart is a bar and someone else works there now.

My heart is in a bar
that feels like someone else's home when I walk into it.
  (*Sorry to intrude. This can't be the right place. It can't be.*)

If I never go back there, does it mean everything's okay?
Does it mean you're still waiting for me
to agree to that date? Does it mean nothing changes
if I stop looking back at it?   Will you still save me a seat?

Tumblr, 2017

Anonymous asked:

Gosh your poetry always makes me feel I love you so much

I MIGHT BE A MEDIOCRE WAITRESS IN THE REAL WORLD BUT PEOPLE ON THE INTERNET REALLY SEEM TO LIKE MY POETRY AND I ABSOLUTELY HAVE TO BELIEVE THAT MEANS SOMETHING

Fragments #20

Sometimes I think I'd put down the pen
if it would give me an easier life.

I could be small and quiet.
I could do that.

—I know I have a heart like a wild thing
with snapping jaws and matted fur
but I'd hang up my hands on hooks for you,
pluck out all of my sharp teeth
for the chance to be
easy.

Give me a collar and I'll sleep on the floor.
Let me belong to somebody
just for a minute.

I know the taste of hunger intimately.

       It is exhausting   to want   to be loved.

2014–2023

[Stars Yell at Woman]   [Woman Yells Back]

Your heart   is starving

and you're so
fucking loud about it

everyone knows
but you.

///

2023

2017

the year I wrote about tenderness
like it was a dark stain on a white shirt.
the year I tried to make it work
and it didn't.

the year I built a life for myself
and then abandoned it.
the year I was scared and predictable.
stole my love letters back.
slept in motels in eighteen different states.

the year I tucked misery under my tongue
but forgot how to swallow it.
the year I spit it up all over the place
and watched our mutual friends sidestep the mess.

> wiped my mouth.
> got back to work.
> paid the bills.
> kept my head down.
> took your bullshit apology
> and fed it to the paper shredder.

the year I was tough again
because it was too risky to be soft.
all bramble and no blackberry.

I turned all of our poems on their heads.

Instagram, 2017

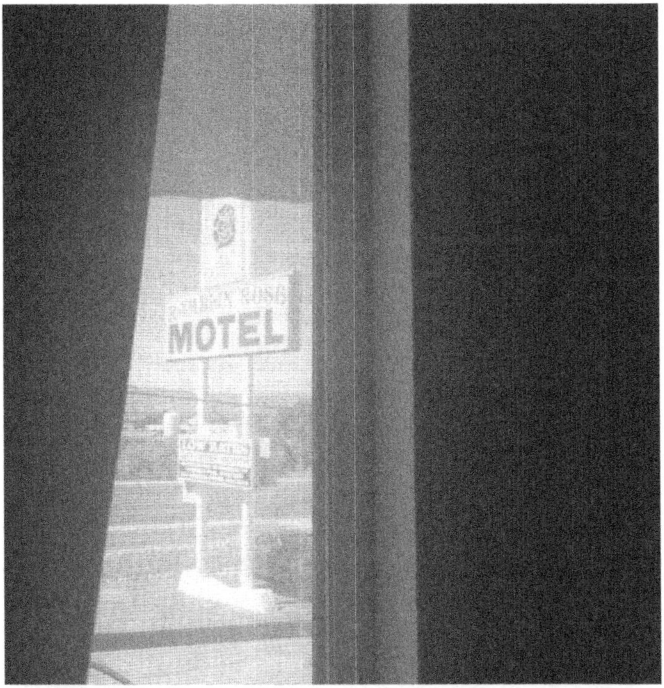
MOTEL

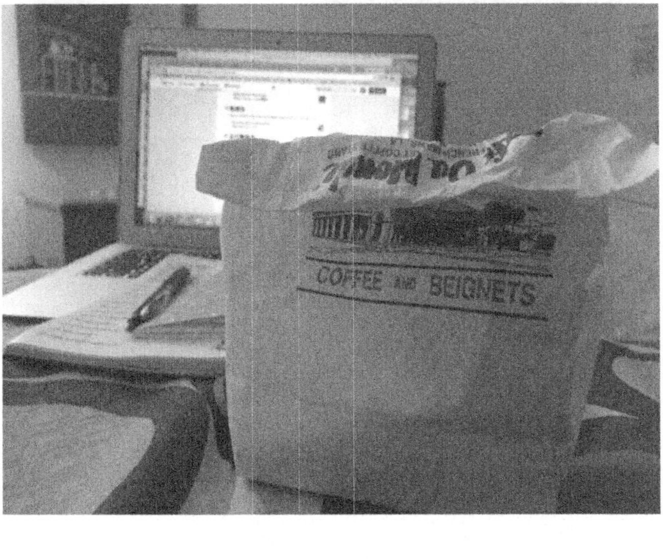
COFFEE AND BEIGNETS

Separation in the American South

It is May
and the nights blend together
like butter and honey.

Nothing is going how I thought it would.

This is last June in reverse. The boxes are filling
themselves. I am sleeping next to the packing tape.
I put my regret into a box and write
Free To A Good Home on the side of it.

The old hurt is spilling out everywhere.

My heart is buzzing again. My heart is a wasp's nest.
My heart is a monument to absence.
A postcard that says: *You were here once,
but you're not anymore.*

All of my dreams are about being weightless.
Leaving the heaviness outside and praying for rain.

I am waiting for someone other than myself
to call this predictable. To tell me it had to go this way.
To say, *I don't know what you really expected.*

Tumblr, 2017

After Cruelty

There is a garden and we are still digging it up.

We peel apart the veins of flora
just to get a closer look
at what makes everything hurt so goddamn much.
We press our fingers down sharp on every thorn
and call it love and art and poetry
and the processing of emotion
as it lends itself to healing.

And I say, *It's tender but isn't it done?*
And you say, *It's tender but isn't it over?*
And then we still write soliloquies
about softening in each other's mouths.
I still ask you to put your hands on me
without washing off any of the dirt.

And you say, *Baby.* And you say, *Honey.* And you say,
Don't you love the way the trees sing when the cicadas are out?

And I am in the garden.
And all the trees are humming.

Tumblr, 2016

Get the vodka out of the freezer. Heat up
leftover Chinese food. Close all the blinds.
Turn the lights off. Practice apologies in
the mirror. Burn some candles around your
heart and summon up all the old ghosts
so you have something to write about
other than her hands and her mouth
and her hands and her mouth and her
hands and her goddamn mouth.

2016 - cut from *Before the First Kiss*

I'LL EAT MY OWN HEART BEFORE I GIVE YOU THE CHANCE

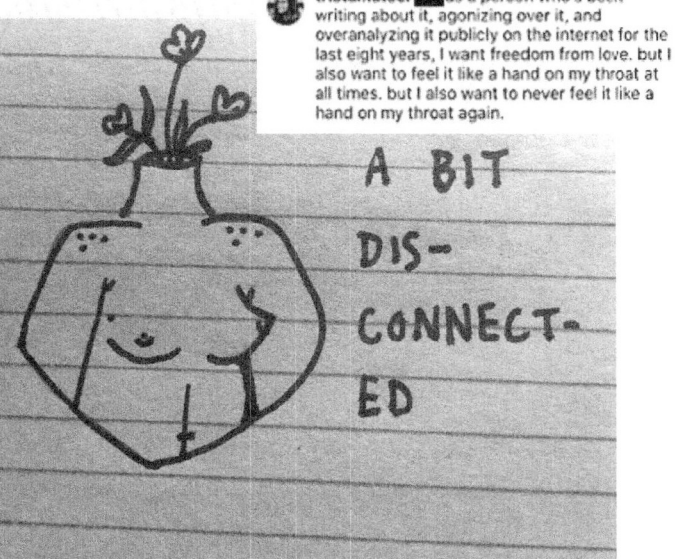

tristamateer as a person who's been writing about it, agonizing over it, and overanalyzing it publicly on the internet for the last eight years, I want freedom from love. but I also want to feel it like a hand on my throat at all times. but I also want to never feel it like a hand on my throat again.

A BIT DIS- CONNECT- ED

Fragments #19

[You are dragging the past around by its ankles.]

    [She's getting tired of you.]

        [This girl is gonna make you bleed.]

    Of course it ended on asphalt.
I chipped my teeth on every poem she wrote about me.

    What kind of chance did we really have,
making each other pay for the mistakes of other lovers?

My   heart is a fisherman's net.
It wants to keep everyone that gets caught inside of it.

    That's just   not sustainable.

2016–2023

You might hate me now
but you loved me first

        to the point of
          no return.

Anonymous said

Sometimes I lose hope in love and then remember you and ▮▮▮ exist.

many others were watching *Your* terrible wild life

Fragments #18

Summer is here
and our love is uncomfortable again   in its quiet way.

       YOU DON'T WANT TO BE LOVED.

       YOU WANT TO BE ADORED.

       YOU WANT THE MEAT OF LOVE

       WITH NONE OF THE BUTCHERING.

    You want to call me
    and tell me that you're in love with me   but

~~there's all this distance and no one willing to cross it.~~
~~Not in a real way. Not in a way that means anything.~~

I drove   across the country
to drink sugar water   out of the palm of your hand

and now I'm sleeping on the couch.

2016–2023

The First Time I Thought About Leaving

It was the September we had our hot water cut off.
I washed my hair in the kitchen sink
and ate oatmeal naked on the couch every morning.
The neighbors across the hall slammed their front door
and opened it again
to start a new argument or finish an old one.
I got used to the sweat dripping down my neck,
Texas heat buzzing late in the season.
I got used to a lot of things.

It was the month you started referring to it
as your apartment again instead of ours.
A little wound every time, a little prayer to my suitcase

[so much time feeling unwanted in my own home]

but I didn't run like they said I would.
I waited it out.

2018

Cohabitation in the American South

It is June and I am knocking down my heart
like a wasp's nest on the front porch,
taking stock of everything that spills out of it,
no longer running from the old hurts,
but looking for a way to catalogue them
before the big move.

This box is for storage and this box is
to be chucked into the reservoir and this box is
for things that are warm and soft and growing.
This box is for pots and pans, this box is
for all the poems I wrote about peaches
before I started hating peaches.
This box is for you.

It's still months off, but I imagine
autumn rolling in and all of the unpacking.
How we will take the box-cutter together
and slice through the packing tape,
upend ourselves in the kitchen of our new apartment.
How we will kiss over the clutter.
How the wasp's nest of my heart will turn
more cocoon, more sturdy,
more protective than predatory.

Until then,
I am out on the porch with a broom handle.
It is June and the days bead up
like condensation on a glass.

Tumblr, 2017

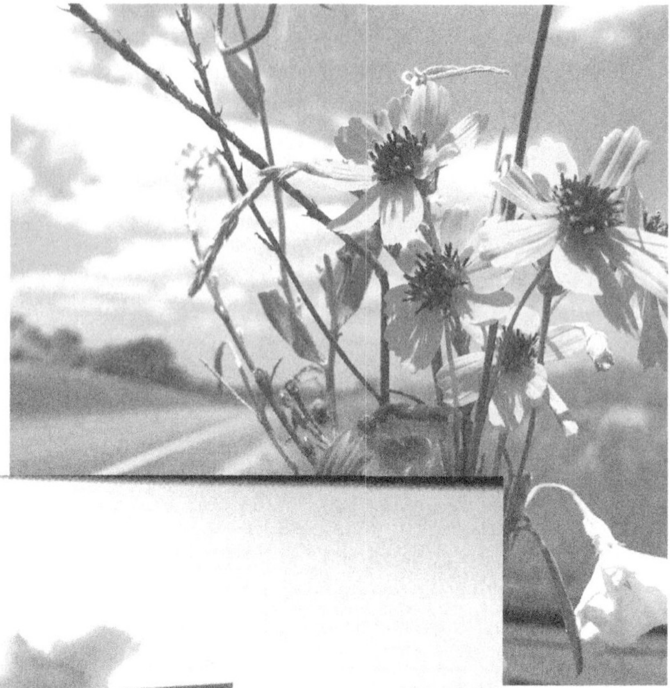

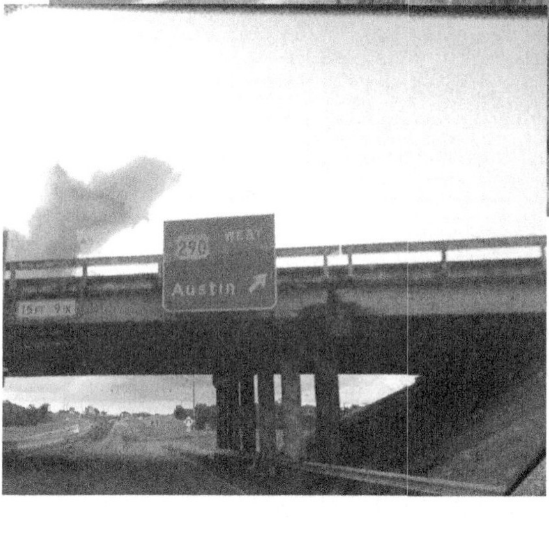

<3

Come to me.
Come to me.

Like Venus in her clam shell,
all I have to offer you is everything.

Tumblr, 2015

spilled my guts on the internet again
        I'm not above being embarrassing

I was underground   when you found me
        now I'm up   so high I can't breathe

2018

2/14

It's February 14th and I owe you a poem,
but all I can think is:

your hands and your mouth and
your hands and oh, god
your mouth.

Tumblr, 2016

In this space right here
that we have made for each other,
you can say anything
and I will not abandon you.
Unwrap the worst things you have done.
Watch me hold them up to the light
and not even flinch.

Tumblr, 2018

Queer Girl Overture

I have this dream where I am not afraid to hold your hand in Texas. This dream where I don't have a visceral reaction to seeing gay pride flags. This dream where I can invite you home for Christmas dinner and my mother is so kind to you. And she asks where you went to school and she doesn't choke on your gender identity and she pulls me aside later to tell me how sweet you are. I have this dream where people on the internet stop changing the pronouns in my poetry. I have this dream where I know exactly what to say when my Southern Baptist relatives ask if I'm dating someone. I have this dream where I don't have to keep coming out over and over. Where people don't think my sexuality is a phase unless I can produce a girlfriend on command. Where people stop asking me who fucks better: men or women. Like those are the only options. Like the answer wouldn't be a gross generalization. I have this dream where people aren't always waiting to say, *Maybe you haven't found the right guy.* Where I don't imagine them jumping out from behind doors and bushes and shower curtains to say, *I hope you get over this in time to have children of your own.* I have this dream where all of my queer representation isn't murdered on TV. I have this dream where my queer friends aren't murdered on the news. I have this dream where I feel safe. In rural Kansas. At my grandparents' house. In a gay bar. At Pride. I have this dream where I only write you love poems and none of them have to say, *I'm so glad we're alive.*

Tumblr, 2016
Aphrodite Made Me Do It, 2019

Fragments #17

I'm angry   at God.
I'm angry   at my mother.
I'm angry   at myself.

I'm angry but this poem is not to say that I am angry.
(This poem, like all poems, is a safe space.)

> This poem
> is not the only place
> I can kiss my girlfriend
> without worrying who's watching,
> but sometimes it feels like it is.

She tastes like honey   and heaven   but

sometimes kissing her
feels like a precursor to violence.

I think about how fast I might have to drop it
every time I reach for her hand.

2016–2023

Fragments #16

So
her voice
is the opposite of a lullaby.
More like a moan in the dark.
She   keeps me up all night.

      She tastes like sweet tea and seven other Texan
cliches / tastes like spurs, without the boots, without
the cowboy. /

      Red dirt, red sky, all blood & blush.
Summer even when it's not. /

She has a heart like a rose at the center of a sticker-bush

&   my heart is so full of maybe,
I can't even get away from it when I sleep.
      In my dreams,   I kiss   with more teeth than lip.

      I can't help myself.   I need this.

She makes me want to ransack my own temple.

I'd suck salt off   her fingers
like a fucking animal.

2015–2023

Fragments #15

YOU as a long drive through the desert, sunset in the Midwest. YOU as a cold glass of water to parched lips.

   (the kindest place I ever wanted to run toward)

curse   every soft, late night I was full of hesitations. every bruise   every anxiety attack and quiet promise

YOU as poet, preacher's daughter, dream girl.

      dream girl again.

Never thought I'd miss Our self-indulgent love poems

I know it is too late to lose my breath over the way your heart grins before it eats /

 and I do it anyway /

2016–2023

More Poems I'm Not Writing

It Was Some Other Girl Who Fucked Everything Up
(Some Other Girl, Not Me)

Seven Reasons I Can't Ask You to Leave Your
Boyfriend for Me

In Defense of Janelle the Florist (I'm Glad the Flowers
Got Delivered / We Were Not Good to Each Other /
I Miss You)

I Know This Makes Me the Asshole in Our Story

Fuck Tenderness I Wish I Could Swallow The Sun

Did This Make You Feel Better?
Because It Didn't Do Anything for Me

Follow-Up Questions for an Old Lover

I Don't Know How to Explain It Other Than to Say
My Own Heart Enjoys Working Against Me

2016
Lines from the cutting room floor of *Before the First Kiss*.

so you glorified love, sang its praises, called it godlike /
but remember us? / be honest

remember your bare feet burnt on sun-soaked asphalt,
all that distance you failed to cross /

remember the timed reminders to take your
medication, recommendations for sleeping pills
whispered over the phone /

remember the way we ripped at each other's throats
when love didn't work the way we wanted it to

/ the months we went hand to hand at each other's
bruises, wept at the sight of flowers left on the wrong
doorstep / carved the soft out of our own stomachs and

fed it to each other like ripe seedless grapes, like

fingers dipped in wine and fish-hooked into mouths /

I called my body a temple when I wanted you to
worship at it, but all you ever offered me was poetry
/ I wanted the fruits of labor / wanted evidence of
action or blood let at the altar / how unholy we turned
out to be, how violent our tongues / look how we
burned with love and watched the flames lick at
everything but each other

Tumblr, 2016   *I've kissed too many poets*

•••oo Sprint 🔗   9:41 AM   ⌐ @ 🔘 ▮▮

⟨ Notes   Done

February 13, 2016, 9:38 AM

This is what happens when two people romanticize each other to the point of fiction/

•oooo Sprint 🔗   10:09 AM   ⌐ @ ▯

⟨ Notes

March 10, 2016, 10:09 AM

we're finally in the same city but you don't want to kiss me anymore

@ the Women of the World Poetry Slam Brooklyn, NY

On Writing Love Poems
(About Multiple People And Sharing
Them On The Internet, Where They Are
Inevitably Found By Everyone I Date)

Fuck the old love poems.
I keep them around as a reminder to do better.

I have written whole books for other people
but the quantity of poetry doesn't measure the love,
just the hurt.

[Redacted], 2016

Trista Mateer · *I Swear Somewhere This Works*

Here I am
knowing the difference
between honey and the bee,

still chasing
what stings.

Instagram, 2019
Artemis Made Me Do It, 2022

Hymn for an Open Mouth

Ask me about the summer
I fell in love with someone
more blackberry bramble than girl.
Aching to be touched
but never talking about the thorns.
   And me, all heavy handed
   and too proud to acknowledge
   the things I'd cut myself on.
   I dreamt about juice
   running down my chin
   for months.

Before the First Kiss, 2016

Wanting Her

The poets say *love*
like it's synonymous with *tender*.
I don't know how to want like that anymore.
Everything is tooth and nail, everything is visceral.
All instinct and no logic.
I compare all my lovers to fruit
so I can rip them apart.
What does that say about how this will end?
Still,

wanting her
feels like stomach ache & fever,
feels like doing the one thing
I know I'm not supposed to,
feels like another brick through my window
but at least I know this one is coming.
There might be fear stuck in my throat
but at least it's coated in honey.

*I was right to be scared
but I'm still glad we tried*

Before the First Kiss, 2016

Fragments #14

Everything ends
                     and that's okay, isn't it?

Aren't you getting tired? Don't your eyes feel heavy?
The day is growing late. The hours are passing.

It's okay to let go of the things that keep you up at night.   You don't have to be miserable forever.

         You don't have to agonize over loss until you die. Something's always dying

         but it doesn't always have to be you.

2018–2023

Personal Reflections on Gender

I used to think girl meant wilting like a rose in the palm of a man's hand / but sometimes it just means thorn / and sometimes it just means wilting into my own hands / sometimes it means blue and elbow tattoos / lawn chairs and birch beer and lightly scented chapstick / sometimes it means being the knife / and the twisted ankle, bloodied lip / sometimes it means not being the poem or the poet / and choking on glitter / kissing someone else's hair / playing jump rope with the binary / and politely or impolitely deconstructing boxes / skin tingling at the thought of being called a pretty boy / or a star cluster / sucking the dirt out from under your own nails just to taste where you came from / without ever having to go back there

Tumblr, 2016
Aphrodite Made Me Do It, 2019

You Will Survive This

I know it can feel like you're
  feral
  and unlovable
  and despicably untouchable

      meant to be alone forever
              and ever,

but you are good
and you are whole
and you are not alone
      or unwanted
        or weak
           or standing at the edge of something

you can't come all the way back from.

Tumblr, 2017

Fragments #13

sweet thing   soft thing   internet sad girl

                                haunting my own house

                    looting the past for grocery money

Girl with   violets in the bags under her eyes.
Girl who used to forgive until it rubbed her heart raw.
    Skinned-knees-on-gravel girl.

       doesn't understand why people keep running
from the blood   of course there's blood

I built my own kingdom on paper, a whole new world
where no one   could keep up with me.

I made a myth out of myself in my youth and
  never found a way   home.

2014–2023

Poem in Which The Moon Breaks Up With Me

Sugar, you never sleep anymore.

                        It's the time difference.
                I don't want to miss your calls.

I'm worried about you.
I hate the idea of you waiting
by the phone. Orbiting
around somebody like that
is no way to live.

I don't think either of us
are really getting what we want.

Not to be cliché,
but maybe we need a little

space.

                    You've got to be fucking kidding me.

[Redacted], 2016

That's Not How This Works

In a universe parallel to this one,
you and I stay up some nights
holding hands in bed,
worrying about all the versions of ourselves
that don't end up together.

Parallel You says, *Somewhere we never even kiss.*
Parallel Me says, *Somewhere we never even touch.*

Parallel You supposes that
the universe
in which we never cross paths
must be a kinder one
than the universe
where we make the effort to love each other
and fail at it so miserably
that we part ways
and never speak again.

Parallel Me says, *That universe doesn't exist.*
Parallel You says, *That's not how this works.*

Instagram, 2016

My twenties
were consumed
by grief
and poetry.

2020

The Kinda Blues

Like sad but not sad enough.
Like attention seeking.
Like *I dunno, man. Most days she seems fine.*
Like laziness and irritation.
Like anxiety but not full-blown panic.
Like not being able to get out of bed for three days but
hey, what's three days?
Like never actually writing the last note,
just imagining the lines.
Like it's more of a river and not an ocean
but as far as I'm concerned
you can drown in either one.

Tumblr, 2015
When the Stars Wrote Back, 2020

Fragments #12

I still don't know how to say half the shit I need to say but you're so   goddamn   patient.

    Thank you for waiting.   Thank you for reading.

I am different more often than I am the same.
I don't know how anybody falls in love with me.
I don't know how anybody keeps up.

        What are you still doing here?

    I am unbearable.

        (And narcissistic.)

I've tried to be so many different things for so many different people. You can't really live that way.
Bent out of shape all the time.

You don't know me. You've just seen inside my head.

We're nothing to each other.

We're closer than lovers.

2014–2023

For You

When You Ask Me How I'm Doing After Reading My Poems Online

The Speaker of the Poems is not having a good day
and everything else is speculation.

>Someone   somewhere in the world
>is having a hell of a time. Someone. Somewhere.

And we have the option to let it not be *Trista Mateer*.

I can only be honest if you're not looking me in the face.

Please don't make me fake it for you here.
Allow me this one place to fall apart,   allegedly.

Instagram, 2020

so death comes
thief in the night
and I'm supposed to act like I haven't been expecting it
like I haven't been counting down the days
for the last three years
like I don't live
with one hand wrapped around a credit card
and the other clutching a plane ticket home
but I wear my shock like a good black dress
and don't make eye contact with the preacher
spend the whole service
making eyes
at the stained-glass windows instead
thinking about how I haven't been to this church
since my great-grandma died
how I ripped my pantyhose on the pew
got my heels stuck in mud at the gravesite
held my brother
while he cried louder than anybody else
I expect this to feel different
but it doesn't
when it's over
I don't settle in with the ache at night
I fly back to Atlanta
pretend nothing happened
I chastise myself for not visiting home enough
like I can always go back
like it's not different this time
like I don't have to carry this

Tumblr, 2016

Polite Conversation

At brunch,
I drink three mimosas
and say his name for the first time
in five years.
I lay my assault down on the table
and my mother doesn't pick it up,
just like she doesn't pick up the poems
that talk about it either.
She says,
He was always such a nice guy.
She says,
He really doesn't seem like the type.
I order a coffee to go.
I don't bring up the root of this poem,
which is not about the man
with his hand on my throat
but about my mother—

her willingness
to look past the things that hurt me
until she becomes one of them.

You tried to talk about it
once, afterwards.
You named it
and laid down until it was over.
You named it
and watched people
walk away from you.
You named it
and felt ashamed.

You still said its name.

The night I was raped,
I walked right past my mother and said nothing.
I was afraid to be dusted for fingerprints.
I was afraid to be called a liar.

Aphrodite Made Me Do It, 2019

Bless all the tales I told on paper.
Bless all the truths I fractured.
Bless all the things I swept under the poem.
Bless the poem for giving me somewhere to hide.

Instagram, 2019

Fragments #11

In this story,   In this story,

you're lying awake at night and
I'm trying to tell you a story   can't you hear it?

specter in a nightgown washing dishes / contemplating
death at the kitchen table /

    Unafraid of a little blood. Unafraid of a lot.

    I'm in love with my anger / my
    war-won body / tense and vicious

/ girl   with a heart   like a beast in a snare

There was always something in me clawing its way out.

2016–2023

The first dragon
she came across
hid itself tight and snug
in the body of a boy
with angry hands.

When she saw fire in his throat,
she did not even think to run.
She did not yet know
that monsters
could look like people.

2016
Scrapped fairy-tale project

~~Once, there was a princess who was not sure that she wanted to be a princess. Or, she wanted a bigger life. Or, she hated fate's design and sought to change it~~

She said, *I do not see myself in this body.*
I wish to be something else entirely.

    And they said, *You want to be a boy.*

And she said, *No. I want to be a knife.*

    Tell us, why? They asked.

And she   screamed.

2016
Scrapped fairy-tale project / part of this was on Instagram

On Masturbating (While Thinking About People Who Don't Love You Anymore)

imagine unhinging your jaw and swallowing everything whole / imagine a touch so tender it sears its prints into you / imagine your lungs filling up at the bottom of the pool / someone spitting into your open mouth and you want it / you want it / you are glad to taste any part of them / your Achilles heel / talk about wanting death from a soft thing / talk about not knowing where to go from here / the clatter in your scatterbrain / you taste yourself and call it testing the waters / you find yourself undressed for the arrow of it / throwing a bone to your weakness / you moan: baby / baby / come back and pull apple cores from the dumpster of me / I swear I throw away all the best cuts

[Redacted], 2016

so love ends and we perish
love ends and we lose ourselves in the fire

or we don't, but we try to

Tumblr, 2016

In the garden again, out of earshot of the house, she says, *Ghosts must have it so easy.* She says there are days she wishes she could pull a sheet over her head before leaving the house.

Thistle Witch speaks to spiders in the garden. She pulls shells out of the dirt. She put a lot of ground between herself and home but you can still smell the sea on her. On a bad day, she rips everything out of the garden, jealous of anything that survives easier than she does. On a good day, she says, *If herbs can grow through the fog in this brick and metal city, maybe I can too.*

When I ask about the state of her heart, she tells me that she doesn't have one. *Not anymore.* Says she misplaced it somewhere on the road, but always makes sure to fill the void in her chest with something to keep the cold out. I don't pry, but I want to and I think she knows it. One morning I wake to find a page from her notebook stuck to the fridge like a grocery list.

> *Things to have in place of a heart:*
>   *An international cell phone plan.*
>   *A well-fed Venus flytrap.*
>   *Open-ended train tickets.*
>   *Broken mirrors.*
>   *A dustpan and a broom.*
>   *Fear of still water.*
>   *Fear of stagnation.*
>   *Fear of wanting something so much*
>   *that you can't leave it behind.*

Tumblr, 2017

between pages. She says nothing is ever real until she writes it down. She takes two full months to write that she lives here now.

Thistle Witch asks me to braid her hair. She tells me that she can do it herself, but, *It feels good to ask for help even if you don't really need it.* She says it's nice to have someone there to anchor her, but she frowns after she says it. Leaves for three weeks and comes home without acknowledging her absence. She just walks back into the flat one morning and upends her purse on the counter. I count twenty-seven different branded sugar packets. She curls up on the rug in the living room like a cat. I don't ask where she's been.

It's not easy to get her to talk about herself. Everything comes out in riddles and half-truths and sometimes lies but she gets upset when I call them that. She says, *Just because it isn't true right now doesn't mean it never was or never will be.* She calls her past a tapestry that is constantly being taken apart and woven back together again. She says the truth is overrated anyway. It's the most boring part of the story.

I say, *I'm like you. Neither of us are from here. Neither of us belong here.* She asks to see my roots, and I don't know what to show her.

Thistle Witch feeds the birds. I've seen them follow her down the street. She said, *It doesn't always hurt to leave things behind. Crumbs and bits of pastry.* She calls it practice for letting go.

Thistle Witch Excerpts

There's a witch in the garden again, smoking hand-rolled cigarettes. The first time I caught her there, she was pulling up everything but the weeds. Out went the tomato plants and the lemongrass. Perennials, up by the roots. When I asked why, she closed her hand hard around a thistle and then released it. Watched it spring back into place and showed me the blood on her palm. She said, *Have you ever seen anything more resilient?*

I didn't ask her name until the third time. She was perched on a rusted lawn chair talking to the fog. She swatted me away and said she didn't have one, but things get lost in translation sometimes. I have come to understand she doesn't have only one name. Calls herself Sea Glass, calls herself Peregrine, calls herself Patron Saint of Leaving and laughs about it. Scatterling. Magpie Woman. I asked what her mother called her and she said, *It sounds so far away.* She said, *If people change, I don't understand why names get stuck.* She called it false advertisement and offered me a sugar packet from the pocket of her large plaid coat.

The next time, she showed up at my front door instead. She had a suitcase, a backpack, and a box of mugs. Now I rent her a room on the second floor but she rarely ever sleeps there. I wander into the kitchen at odd hours to find her rolling cigarettes and making tea, hanging herbs up to dry, paging through old notebooks. One has moss hanging out of it, one leaks all over the kitchen table every time it's closed. She says these are normal setbacks when you're tasked with collecting a life

The Year of Smooth Dishonesty

Low light & soft focus. Hard with the edges shaved off. Hard but toned down for a broader audience.

The year you wrote about flowers and meant blood,

the year you were quiet about everything that hurt.

The string of apartments with bad roommates, the suitcase always packed on the bedroom floor, all that love you kept talking about but didn't want to fight for

        and still, it spread out sticky all over everything, connected your mouth to the lamplight, handwritten notes to the internet, poetry to the rent check.

The year you lived off of love but didn't live in it,

the year loneliness permeated everything and you didn't open your mouth to tell anyone, because how could they   not know?

[Redacted], 2016

Now That You Mention It

Sorry for being a creature of the night.

Sorry for obsessing over love for my entire life.
       Sorry for other things.

I lied when I said we were basically roommates and not lovers. I lied when I said you meant nothing to me.

       (I make a liar out of myself on paper all the time.)

I don't want to be good and Mary said that's fine.

Can you do me a favor? Can you

       rinse out my skull
       and fill it with flowers

and go around telling everyone how very sorry

       I am

             for the mess?

2021

Trista Mateer · *I Swear Somewhere This Works*

It would be a shame
to look back on this
and (out of bitterness)
not call it love.

We both know what it was

Tumblr, 2015
Honeybee 2nd edition, 2018

A Month of Not Kissing You
March 1-March 31 2015

I'm still trying to make something
out of your absence.

Anonymous asked:

What inspired you to do a month of not kissing you

tristamateer answered:

I'm not going to get into details, but I wanted to kiss someone and I couldn't. So I wanted to show them all the love they were missing out on. And I wanted to make that whole month of hurting something I could ball up and throw away or frame and stare at. I wanted to be able to touch it. I wanted to be able to rip it up. I wanted something to point at when people asked me how I was doing.

2015, Tumblr
Materials: sketchbook paper, assorted lipstick, Sharpie, terrible phone camera

a month of
not kissing you

That quiet dream.   That inevitable future.

Part of me was so sure, so fucking sure
that you were   THE ONE   on a long list of people
who hadn't come close.

That part of me still wakes up thinking about you.

Still chokes on your absence.
Still tries to hate-fuck you out of her head.

She's not even sad so much as angry and it's the anger
       I don't know what to do with.

I've done so much fucked-up shit just to try
and let you go,
I'm afraid that if I ever make it back to California

I won't be the same girl you fell in love with.

      Maybe that's okay.
      Maybe I forgive you.

                        Maybe I don't.

Tumblr, 2015

So Long, Charlotte

I never want you to read this poem.

I never want you to know that I'm still hanging onto the way you drove me off. That I saved all your voicemails. That I still have that car park ticket from The Golden Gate pressed into the front of my wallet.

Sometimes I feel like meeting you was a dream, like

some other girl slipped into a stranger's hot tub and took her bra off and tried to kiss you.

How could that be real?

> Your voice next to me, your voice across
> the ocean, your voice in my head.

When you touch me
it feels like watching the sun set over a bridge
I used to want to jump from.

> When you don't touch me, it still feels like
> being on that bridge.

I don't know how
our bodies   got so used

                 to the space between them.

I keep trying out different ways to say goodbye
    to the idea of us.

Flushed Cheeks & Soft Exclamations

how long do you think it takes someone to recognize a soulmate? two hours? three? when I was sitting in that train station, did you know I never once thought that you might not show up? did you know you're the reason gin keeps sneaking into my poetry? and how come we both have to write poetry to feel clean? and can we go back to the museum so I can view you next to the art? and should I be doing more on the bad days? what good intentions don't get swallowed up by distance? do you really think it's true, about the stars and how I found you? did you know I'd snuff them out if I could? if it meant there'd be nothing star-crossed about this? tell me again how long you think it takes someone to recognize a soulmate? one night? two? the amount of time it takes you to buy sugar and run home to put the kettle on?

Lost my heart to a Glasgow girl

[Redacted], 2016

I was going to write you a poem
        but I just ended up crying
        about how much I love you
        and how far I am from you
        and how

            really

everything we say to each other is poetry.

2016, Tumblr

Trista Mateer · *I Swear Somewhere This Works*

[Woman Yells at Stars]   [Stars Yell Back]

Who said
it had to hurt this much
to make good art?

/ /

                                            Who said you're
                                         making good art?

[Redacted], 2016

[woman yells at stars]

Delivered

[stars don't give a single fuck]

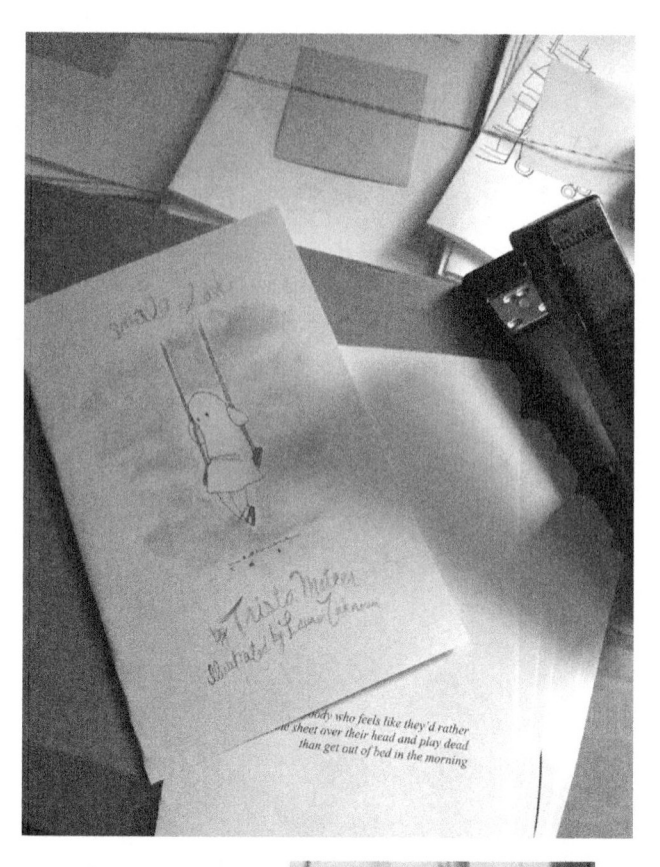

body who feels like they'd rather
the sheet over their head and play dead
than get out of bed in the morning

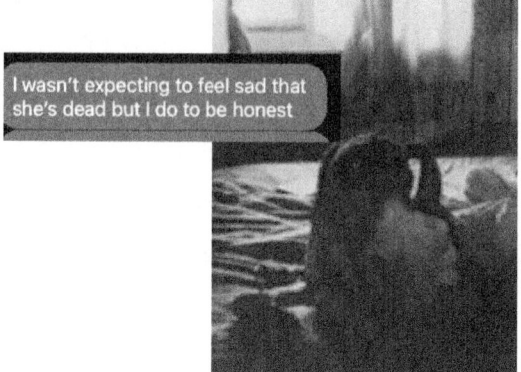

> I wasn't expecting to feel sad that she's dead but I do to be honest

Small Ghost Haunts Herself

once / she tried to draw a self-portrait
but couldn't remember what she looked like

she makes things so people know she's still here / she
makes things so she knows she's still here / once
she stood at the foot of your bed / whispered
poetry while you were sleeping

there's something about emptying her guts out to
people who don't ask for her name that doesn't
feel good   but it feels okay

she keeps crying over people who don't exist anymore
or people who don't matter anymore   maybe both

she can't remember
when she started digging her own grave
but now she can't stop hovering over it

         aren't i too old to be this sad?

she paces the kitchen
     walks past a new set of   knives over and over
has to remind herself twice in the span of five minutes

     you belong here   *you belong here*

(excerpts) *Small Ghost*, 2015

Fragments #10

I still forget we're not even friends.   You're still the first person I want to share new things with.

      I used to be washed away with grief at the sound of your name, but now there's just the dull ache of memory.

          Time doesn't heal wounds
      but it helps you forget all the blood.

I'm   tired of mourning what's not even dead

but isn't it dead? Didn't something die here?

I know you're out there somewhere and the thought of that is almost too much to bear. Do you remember what we were? How are you living without me? How am I living without you?

      Remarkable.
      Astonishing.

I never thought I'd see the day.

I was so sure   the absence of your love would kill me.

2014–2023

We're both crying in my flat again
but it's not about each other.
It's about weakness. Yours and mine.
Your ability to get on a plane and sleep in my bed.
My ability to let you.
How we touch and it means nothing
but we do it anyway.
A force of habit
like flicking the ash off a cigarette
or removing your shoes by the door.
I am the motion you go through
when you can't find another good bed to die in.
Yours are the hands I want on my throat,
but only when you're gone.
Only when they're not really your hands.
Just the memory of pressure.

Tumblr, 2017

Lonely?
Well, I never

        I never

We all
Want to die for love,
Ophelia

        You didn't need to be so dramatic

I have stones in my pockets   too

So does every other woman

2023

Fragments #9

Not sure   what to say about love anymore.
It feels so far away.

If love has a face, I don't remember it.
I don't know   if I'll be a poet forever.

                                        I don't know   what else to be.

Despite everything,

        I still want to talk about love.
        The way it stays the same. The way it changes.

2016–2023

Robin,

To end up with a man who wanted you
but wanted nothing to do with your choices,
cared nothing for all the times you said NO,
set up a string quartet and roses
in your living room
anyway, a man
who mishandled you start to finish
in the name of romance and the grand gesture—

Robin, to end up with a man
more in love with the idea of love than with you
must seem like some kind of cosmic betrayal,
must seem so season one
pre–All That Character Development.

I know that after years of the same tired back and forth,
it must be so easy to mistake poor scripting for fate.
But, listen to me: fuck the grand gesture.
Robin, FUCK THE BLUE FRENCH HORN.

He does not always deserve to Get The Girl
just because he wants the girl.

Sometimes the girl gets to drink a neat scotch
and pile into bed with her five dogs
comfortable, happy, and alone.

Robin, sometimes the girl gets herself.

Tumblr, 2017

Make small attempts at tenderness.

2016

Everything But The Rind

a discarded citrus peel
resting on the kitchen counter / so comfortable

being both beautiful and unwanted / so unbothered

by the lack of hands on it / so unlike   this body /

and the way it catalogs every day
it hasn't been touched / but
doesn't know what to do with the number

    / just knows it doesn't feel like a body
    / when it's not being used by someone outside of it

Tumblr, 2017

Rachel,

The world is full of men
who would pick you apart and call it kindness.
Men who would criticize you down to your ankles
and then say that you worry too much
about your appearance.

Men who would consider themselves
more important than your career goals
but also belittle you for not having career goals.
Men who would complain about your past
and then put themselves in the way of your future.

The world is full of men
who confuse obsession with romance.

Men who would make a meal
out of your core and call it love.

Men who would lay your flaws out like a banquet
and then shove them in your face.

Men who would say they love you in spite of *you*.

Rachel, the world is full of Ross Gellers.

Rachel, get on the plane.

Tumblr, 2015

In Which Jordan Poremski Is Just a Boy

Somewhere in New York State is a boy with sunflowers for hands. Or there isn't, but I thought there might be. There are at least twelve ways to make a myth out of a man but there's only one good way to tend to something after you plant it. I expected you to know this. You had such a knack for making things grow in me.

Somewhere in New York State is a girl drowning in a metaphor or thinking about a crosswalk or trying to figure out the difference between a partner and a muse, and she's coming up empty-handed because you can't look her in the face anymore. Aren't you supposed to wave before you cross the street to avoid me?

What is every poem about if not this?

You needed to love something other than yourself to feel alive and it wasn't me. So you're human. So you're more boy than myth and all the flowers are left wilting.

I named something in my garden after you and it died.

I put your name in this poem and it ended.

Tumblr, 2017

For Caitlin Conlon

Fragments #8

I slept incredibly well before I met you.

I've never sat with absence like this before.
    It melts on the tongue like a peppermint.

      These are the long months when the poems all come out misshapen and every ghost story sounds like a love note if I use the right tone of voice.

    I don't know a thing about quiet desperation.
      I'm sorry if I embarrassed you.

        The poet writes almost exclusively about love even though she's not sure it really exists. The poet emotionally tortures herself for art. The poet emotionally tortures other people for art. The poet is having trouble making peace with privacy. The poet wrote a whole book about letting things go and still doesn't know how to let a single thing go.

These days I spend a lot of time thinking about sex
and different ways to die
and never really loving anybody in particular.

2016–2023

You never met me halfway
but I still sat out like taffy under a heat lamp.
I still turned myself inside out for someone else.
There are good bits to this too.
I swear it's not all fucked up.
I swear it's not all fabricated.
It was the truth at some point.
Or I wanted it to be.
Or it could have been.
Or I just got mixed up
writing about different people
who looked a lot like us
but weren't afraid to touch each other.

2018

So yes, I love you,
but it doesn't mean anything.
I am still greedy, living on excess,
a mouth running red
with cherry juice.

And you
are just running.

Tumblr, 2015

All Those Coffee Cup Metaphors My Editor Complained About

I'm sorry for what this has been,
this dirty love-making, pulling you through the mud
just to see you leave a stain on something. For the teeth
never knocking against each other but always grabbing
hold of something. For the tired eyes and sore throats,
chipped voices, bad lines. The begging and the leaving
and the coming back to leave again.

I'm sorry for the poems.
All the shouting I did about your mouth.

Tumblr, 2016

Fragments #7

I'm afraid of love. I'm afraid of other things.

One day
I will stop panicking when I can't perfectly remember the pitch of your voice or the curve of your jawline.

I'm afraid   of forgetting.

Look, I'm not saying I'm still in love with you or anything. Things can be important even though they're not important in the same way anymore. You still occupy space inside of me somewhere.
    I'm not still in love with you or anything but

I just hate that life moves on without us sometimes.

(*I still remember you.*)   (*I still remember you.*)

There are other truths but these are   ours.

2014–2023

Trista Mateer · *I Swear Somewhere This Works*

I feel most like myself
when I am washing blood off my hands
in the shower; and I hope
whatever is eating you alive
does it as slowly
as possible.

I know it doesn't sound like it,
but this is a love poem,
this is a love poem,
this is a love poem

until it isn't anymore.

Tumblr, 2016

Trista Mateer · *I Swear Somewhere This Works*

This is an apology
for the things I have to say about us

to get over us.

Tumblr, 2016

Trista Mateer @tristamateer 4/21/16
INSTEAD OF WRITING OUR BREAKUP POEM, I tell Twitter how much I miss you in the middle of the night.

< Sent   **definitely a post script**

This is just to say, I'm sorry for not letting go sooner. I still think about you. Maybe not in the same way. But I do think about you. I always hope you're well. I always hope you're happy. I've been trying to write our "breakup poem" for eight months now. Here's the hang up: sometimes things don't break, they just end.

Instead of Writing Our Breakup Poem

I buy four new books of poetry and black out
the poems that remind me of you. I start feeding
my Neopets again. I keep notes on how long
it takes my succulents to die without water.

I think a lot about absence and the heart. I test
the weight of words like *foolishness* and *devotion*
on my tongue. I am rough with the memory of you.

I stop masturbating because it makes me cry.
I make bad art and keep it to myself. I make bad art
and share it with the internet.

I strip down to my underwear and eat alone in my bed.
I think, *This is what loneliness feels like*. And I let myself
sink into it. I practice ways to disappear completely.

I yell at the stars. I play devil's advocate with myself.
I clip coupons and daydream about decorating
an apartment you've never set foot in.

I stare a lot at my ceiling thinking about how I could
change cities and the ghost of your hands would still
follow me everywhere. I change cities anyway.

Tumblr and Twitter, 2015
(excerpts) *Instead of Writing Our Breakup Poem*, 2016

Relationship Postscript

I'm sad but I still want to fuck you.
Spent ten hours crying next to a stranger
over the Atlantic, couldn't stop thinking
about your skin pressed under my fingertips,
or the way your mouth tastes,
or the way one of us is always leaving the other.

And I want to fuck you like only the past fucks you.

And I want to fuck you like you fucked me.

I want to run home and
pull the sheets over my own head,
      never move again
           never think about the way we moved again.

I'm sorry I called myself a dog.

I'm not sorry I called you a coward.

Tumblr, 2015

I made juice
out of every orange
I wrote your name on
and you cringed at the
pulp. It's a joke, how
sweet I thought
you'd taste in my bed.

[Redacted], 2016

Excuses, Excuses

You have run off and taken my anger with you.
Zeus drawing lines in the sand
with his lightning bolts
because he cannot find a reason to throw them;
I think you're a coward.
I think other poets have written this poem.
I think other men have run off the same way
but it never really feels the same.
Each new absence a fresh burn.
A grazed knee. A paper cut. A plane crash.

Tumblr, 2015

Observations After The Fact

i. So I never pressed my palms
against the thing that broke me.

So the ending is small and unglamorous.

So, okay.

ii. The best part about this city
is that it is so big, you can break my heart in it
and never have to worry about seeing me
on your morning train.

iii. I don't get to come back from this.
I never get to be the person I was before I met you.
(Or didn't meet you.)
She sat by the phone but I got on the plane
and there's no coming back from that.
There are some things you never get to be again.

Tumblr, 2015

Fragments #6

So, okay.   I should have seen the signs.

I'm writing another love poem because
I don't know
how to write about The Bad Stuff yet.

    The Crying   The Leaving   The Giving Up

how could you   how could you actually do this?

You graffitied your name all over my heart
and then stood me up at the airport.

IN ANOTHER LIFE, you meet me at the arrivals gate

but
IN THIS LIFE,

    you're spineless and I'm a bitch and
    everyone is in on the joke.

2015–2023

Waiting

I told you I did not want to be that girl.
That wait around girl. That call-me-back-girl.

    Please call me back.

Lover, I am the most impatient loser on the planet.

Lover, I am lonely for you only.

Lover, lover.

    I don't know how to do this.

Tonight you could strike a match on me.
I have a mouth made of kindling.

Tumblr, 2014

Fragments #5

You have EXIT sign lips.
Something I want to run toward in case of emergency.
And everything is an emergency. Lover,
        come lay your hands on me.

I know there's nothing romantic about plane tickets.
Tell me you want to buy them anyway.

I don't want to write another poem
about being far away from you.

2013–2023

Laugh Lines

I am always moving toward you.
On my bad days, I say to myself: *then you.*
Sure, this now. But then you.

I will keep tossing myself life lines.
I will keep writing myself afloat
until I don't have to write a poem
for every mile marker
from here to California.

You and I together is the most foolish thing
I've ever hoped for. You and I apart is more foolish.
Sometimes, I want to apologize
for wanting you out loud.
(All these fucking poems!)
Too many people know the reasons
I'm going to have laugh lines.
(I didn't mean to tell them everything.)

Sometimes, instead of distanced pillow talk,
I want to curl up with the phone
and read you poetry.
Instead, we just talk about it.
You say, *Honey, how was your day?*
And I say, *Today I wrote another poem*
about your coffee cup mouth
and all the ways you keep me up at night.
I hear a sigh in your smile.
You're still too far away.

Tumblr, 2014
The Dogs I Have Kissed, 2015

The Most Magnificent Pastime

He said, *I never want to pull out of you*
and I think I fell in love. What a fucked-up thing to do.
And this wasn't supposed to be a fucked-up poem
but it's turning into a fucked-up poem
because I haven't been able to come in three years
without thinking of his hips sliding into mine:

like first base,
like second base,
like third base,
like home.

The Dogs I Have Kissed, 2015

Oranges

I wake up in the middle of the night
and I text you things like, *Why aren't you in my bed?*
Come eat a bowl of oranges off of me.
I don't know what this means.
I don't even know what I'm trying to say.

Something about you and me in bed
with sticky fingers
appeals to me even in half-sleep.

Maybe oranges are a metaphor for life.
Maybe I still don't know how many seeds
I'm gonna find in you.
Maybe oranges are just supposed to mean
summer heat
because I'm sick of all this cold.
All this distance.
Maybe it doesn't matter.

Maybe the only thing that means something
is that I am always waking up in the middle of the night
and reaching out to you.

You with those hands.
You with that mouth.

Tumblr, 2014
The Dogs I Have Kissed, 2015

You say, *Here is a casual reminder that I adore you*

and I say, *Be not-casual about it. Adore me un-casually.*
Pretend it's really as big as it feels.

Sometimes I sound too much like a poet.

If there is going to be a sweaty body
panting over top of mine,
I want it to be yours. Cup my breast and call me sugar.
Think about remembering to buy coffee
when you're inside of me.

This is a love poem.

This is a love poem and

I know it's never really as big as it feels.
Someone looking in from the outside
will always see something
unremarkable. I'm okay with that.
Watch me misplace my metaphors.

Watch me put down my pen long enough
to slide into bed with you and press
my cold feet up against
your warm legs.

This is still a love poem.

Tumblr, 2015

Improper Emergency Procedure

You have more fucking fault lines than California,
but I'd still settle somewhere along your spine
if you'd take the time to stop shifting for a moment.
I'm not afraid of the ground moving under my feet,
but I'm a little worried about your tectonic plates
grinding up against mine in a way
that sends people running for door frames.

Tumblr, 2013
The Dogs I Have Kissed, 2015

I thought about fucking you for my entire flight.

I wonder if I'll ever be able to travel without wishing you were there to meet me on the other side.

but I am still missing you

2013

Little Matchstick Girl

Have you ever noticed how wanting
burns you up
from the inside out?

Like, one moment I am whole,

but then I hear
your voice on the phone

and I swear to God
three blocks away from here
they can smell smoke.

Tumblr, 2014
The Dogs I Have Kissed, 2015

Hometown Gothic

Somewhere, a watched pot refuses to boil
but not here.

In this town
the water runs hot.
The blood runs hot too
and it runs through everything.

Town like a needle, like a lighter, like a bottle.
Town like a fever dream
everyone is trying to wake up from.
Town like a corn maze almost nobody
finds their way out of.

We've all dug a grave or two
just to see what it would feel like to stay.

[screams]

Poetry Is Undead, 2018

~~ONCE UPON A TIME~~
~~THERE LIVED A GIRL~~
~~WHO LOVED NOTHING~~

~~ONCE UPON A TIME,~~
~~IN A COLD AND DESOLATE PLACE~~
~~THERE LIVED A GIRL~~

~~ONCE UPON A TIME~~
~~THERE LIVED A GIRL~~
~~WHO WAS TAUGHT TO BELIEVE~~
~~IN THE POWER OF~~
~~CLOSING ONESELF OFF~~
~~FROM LOVE~~
~~AND HOLDING AS STILL~~
~~AS POSSIBLE~~

THIS IS A STORY ABOUT
HAPPY ENDINGS
AND LIKE ALL STORIES ABOUT
HAPPY ENDINGS

IT BEGINS

A LITTLE ROUGH

The Birth of Thistle Witch

I ask Thistle Witch where she's from and she says,

>*I rolled right out of the sea one day. Well, I was caught in a fishing net. Actually, I came in with the tide.* She says, *I crawled out of the mouth of a man who did my mother wrong. There's nothing left of him.* She says, *I come from Wastelands, Hex Fields, Hell Pits.* She says, *I was born during a Blackberry Winter. Coldest on record.* She says, *I came down from the mountains. The north wind dropped me off.* She says, *I was put together in a stew pot. No, a cauldron. No, a crab boil.* She says, *I walked full-grown out of a swamp and have been looking for solid ground ever since.* She says, *Like all divine things, man had no part in my creation.* She mumbles something halfway-kind about her mother and then takes it back. She says, *We worked hard to make ends meet and didn't always.* She says, *When I left, I didn't know where I was going, just knew it had to be better than where I started.*

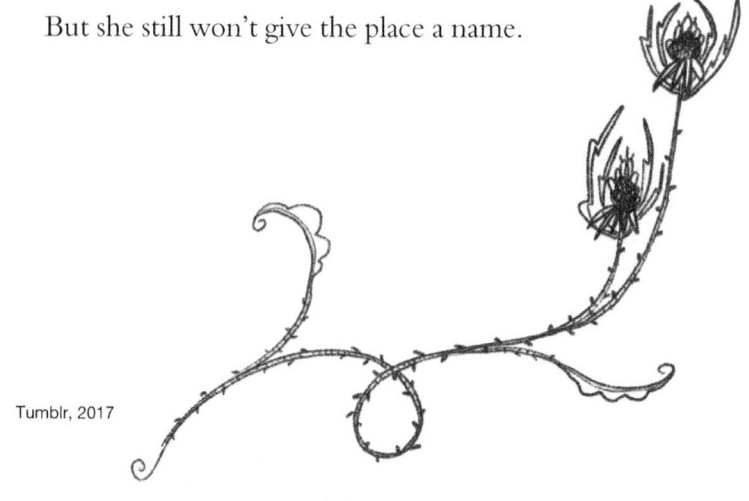

But she still won't give the place a name.

Tumblr, 2017

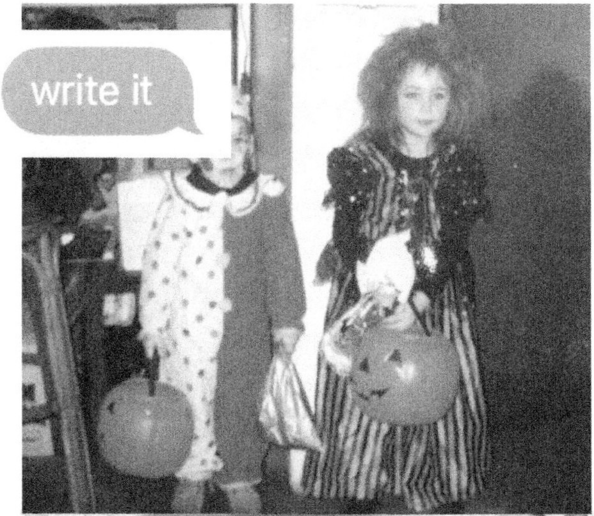
write it

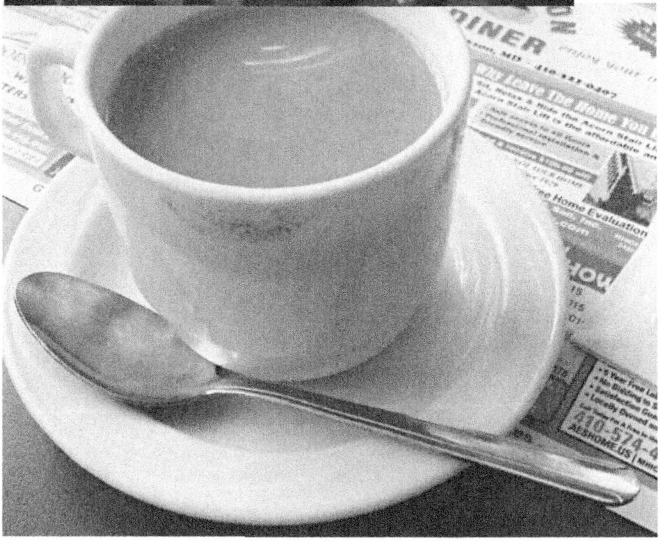
DINER

This doesn't get to kill me.
I rise from the ashes in my free time.
I start over just because I can.

2019 – cut from *Aphrodite Made Me Do It*

Fragments #4

When the Supreme Court ruling
[for marriage equality] comes through,

>I sob until I dry-heave in the lime green
>bathroom of my childhood home.
>
>I picture your hand with my ring on it.
>
>I picture your hand with my ring on it.
>
>I picture your hand with my ring on it.

My mother   asks if I've heard the news.

She says, *I support you because you're my daughter
but I don't agree with it and I don't think it's right.*

>I say, *Then you don't really support me.*
>And she doesn't say anything.

2014-2023

Fragments #3

So you're engaged   So what?
        I skipped all five stages of grief,   I went right to
                [a woman's slow descent into madness]

When I think of our separate futures, I   remember
us   as   girls together
laying in a cornfield, talking about   poetry
writing letters to Ophelia   tasting each other
playing best friends to lovers
asking God what was wrong with us.   (*Nothing.*)

Everything feels so small in your absence.
        My other half.   My broken promise.

I keep   yelling at God.
I   keep trying to picture your hand with someone
else's ring on it. You are getting married in 11 days and

I should have told someone   what he did to you.

I'm sorry I missed the wedding.
I never got an invitation.
        I'm sorry we couldn't save each other.
        We went about it in the worst ways.

I forgive you and   I don't forgive you.   (*Forgive Me.*)
I hope you never call   unless you need to.

2014–2023

If I'd never met you, my life would have been

easier /

    emptier /

        I wouldn't have been a poet.

2018

Even though we were making plans for next week,
I knew I'd never see you again.
I am familiar with leaving. I know its tells:
the way you wouldn't put your hands back on me
or look me in the eye when we said our goodbyes.
You talked your way out of a hug
and I let you.
I spent most of that night looking at your mouth
and wondering why I ever wanted it back on my skin.

2013

Fragments #2

You   made me want to write poetry again.

I needed a god to believe in and it couldn't be me this time / it couldn't be God either obviously / so it's you /

and you said, *My soul will be chasing yours forever*

we're soulmates, you and I, but that doesn't mean it works

You told me that love meant giving and giving
    but at some point, all the plants drown.

You never told me that part.   I wouldn't have agreed.

    wish you were here   wish I was dead

I'd still throw myself mouth-open into the ocean
for the chance to drown somewhere you might see it.

Even on the months I forget to pay my credit card bills,
I still remember to check your horoscope.

    One day   I will not remember
    why I wrote all of these poems.

2013–2023

Fragments #1

*(You knew it was   going to hurt
and you did it anyway. That's just like you.)*

Even now,

when someone asks me about love, I think of your teeth. I think I'm stuck in them. Or I want to be stuck in them. Or I want to be in your mouth. Or,

you get the idea.

So, that's it?
It's tender but it's done?
     It's really over this time?

(You knew it was   going to hurt.)

Why then
all the singing and wailing   in my heart?

(That's just like you.)

2013–2023

Snapchat, 2014

Snapchat, 2014

When I was young
I ran right into
my grandma's menthol cigarette;
I still have the mark to prove it.

I think about this
every time
I imagine your lips on my skin.

Tumblr, 2013

I Swear Somewhere This Works

In a parallel universe or another world
or a different life,

we sit across from each other

at the kitchen table

and go over
the grocery
list.

The Dogs I Have Kissed, 2015

Maybe When I Am Older

I will learn to love without smothering

without walls
and without hard edges.

I'm still not sure there is a right way to do this.

2013
Honeybee 1st edition, 2014

It's So Close Now

We are treading lightly
on the edge of things.

    And I want you to know
    that in spite of it all,

    I loved you fiercely.

Tumblr, 2013
Honeybee 1st edition, 2014

I still remember you
as a little girl
who overwaters plants
because she doesn't know
when to stop giving.

Tumblr, 2015
Honeybee 2nd edition 2018

Trista Mateer · *I Swear Somewhere This Works*

I have a postcard mouth.
All it ever says is:
Wish you were here.

Honeybee 1st edition, 2014
Honeybee 2nd edition, 2018

Consider my body a canvas,
your tongue a brush.
You know how I feel about
blank pages,
open spaces.

Emptiness is there for you to fill it.

You have a lot of
catching up
to do.

Tumblr, 2014

Trista Mateer · *I Swear Somewhere This Works*

Dear,

I don't expect.
I hope. I hope.

Thank you.

Stay safe. Take care.

xoxo

Tumblr, 2014
Love Letter Blackout

Wednesday 11th Jan, 2011

Dear ~~███~~,

~~[crossed out lines]~~ don't expect. ~~[crossed out]~~

~~[crossed out paragraph]~~

I hope. ~~[crossed out]~~ I hope. ~~[crossed out]~~

~~[crossed out]~~ thank you. ~~[crossed out]~~ stay safe. ~~[crossed out]~~ and take care.

~~[crossed out]~~
xoxo.

My ~~darling~~, darling ~~sweetheart~~, sweetheart, ~~love~~,

You ~~~~ and you
~~~~

~~~~

And ~~~~

~~~~

~~~~

~~~~ always
~~~~

Trista Mateer · *I Swear Somewhere This Works*

My darling sweetheart,

You
and you
and you;

always.

Tumblr, 2014
Love Letter Blackout

Trista Mateer · *I Swear Somewhere This Works*

please
tell me which part of yourself
you hate the most
so I know exactly where to plant my lips
every time I see you

Tumblr, 2013

*My first viral poem.
Went around the internet
as a dick joke.
Everyone starts somewhere.*

You Are My Moving Forward

How many people have told you that you feel like
Coming Home? I'm sure you've been somebody's
Shelter, somebody's Summertime, somebody's
Everything before you were anything to me.

You don't remind me of home.
You don't remind me of honeysuckles or
fried green tomatoes or twisted ankles.
You don't remind me of running back
toward anything.

You are not safe walls to hide behind.
You are everything on the other side.

The Dogs I Have Kissed, 2015

Questions for Small Town Girls (Who Like Kissing Girls)

If her mother brings up Leviticus
in polite conversation
and my mother laughs
when she hears the word bisexual,
how much room do we have to breathe
in the middle?

Is it me that makes this wrong
or is it my body
or is it what I want to do with my body?

How do you effectively hold onto something
that you don't want other people to see in your hands?

What if I want other people to see it?

Honeybee 2nd edition, 2018

Early Mechanics of Want

You and strawberries on a lunch break,
kindest excuse for heart palpitations.
Chapstick daydream
on the other side of the table.

On our last day of class, I ask
for your number
but I don't know what to do with it.
So much opportunity folded up on notebook paper
in the pocket of my jeans.
So much pressure, I almost
put it through the spin cycle on purpose.

For Alyssa
forever ago

Tumblr, 2017

She is my creation myth.

Before her,
there was nothing.

And The Interviewer Asks:
Why Did You Start Writing Poetry?

The world was closing in for me.

I needed a door
and I found a window big enough to crawl through.

> What else was I supposed to do?

life was hell / poetry helped

In This Story

You read me your favorite poems and we smash our bodies together when the heat is off but you still aren't in love with me. In this story, you say that you're in love with me and the words are so empty they float when I take them to the river. You told me, once, there was a man who left his sadness in the river and I tried to do the same thing but it didn't work for me.

In this story, things don't usually work for me. Most of the opportunities are missed ones and all of the love poems are gaudy and unfinished. I try to dry flowers and the cat eats them. I go down to the river again and can't find my way home.

There is a woman in our bed and I think she is supposed to be me, but she rarely ever feels like me. You and this woman touch your ankles together under the bedsheets and it passes for intimacy the way almost anything passes for water when the well's run dry or you've misplaced the river.

The river comes up a lot in this story because it is being told from the perspective of someone drowning.

Everything is already underwater.

Tumblr, 2017

I Swear Somewhere This Works

Come here.   Remember with me.

We are old friends
	telling old stories.

I know you've heard this one before.

Thank you for listening, anyway.

A Note From the Author:
On Fragments

  Web-weaving is a term coined by Tumblr blogger Oumaima (to my knowledge) circa 2019, referring to the act of collecting and comparing different pieces of art and literature online, presented together in a sort of collage or carousel. Often these "web weaves" involve bits of poetry, pieces of movie dialogue, film stills, paintings, memes, and other pop culture references all containing some kind of through-line (a similar topic or theme or style).
  As someone who's been writing online for as long as I have, I've seen my poetry used in a multitude of these types of transformative works, from mood boards to fan edits and everything in between. Still, there's something about starting to read a web weave and coming across my own work that always catches me off guard. And then to see it paired with my ex-lovers work, my old friends and colleagues, the people I grew up writing with on Tumblr. The past is inescapable when you write all of it down.

  Over the years, I have written so many lines about the same things, the same feelings, the same people. Allow me to lift the curtain, just for a minute, and string them together.

  Inspired by web weaves, poems you see titled "Fragments" are created from repurposed lines of my existing work. As such, they are credited to a span of years instead of a single year.

Reading these selections of Trista Mateer's work is a crash course in her incredible career as a writer and artist. Weaving between all of her published works and excerpts that have only ever lived online, Mateer creates a narrative of love, loss, and finding yourself somewhere in the aftermath, battered and bruised but still here. You're given the opportunity to acknowledge her roots, the very first seedlings of poems posted on the internet, then marvel at the tree that's grown since in pieces from recent collections like *girl, isolated* and *When the Stars Wrote Back*.

Though many of the poets that came up on Tumblr are no longer active on the website, their impact on art, the online poetry community, and young people everywhere has endured. What this retrospective demonstrates is that Trista Mateer's work helped define a generation of writers that were tired of the bullshit and just wanted to say how they felt, loudly and with reckless abandon. After reading these poems, you might be inspired to do the same.

—Caitlin Conlon,
Author of *The Surrender Theory*

I first discovered Trista Mateer on Tumblr in 2015. Or, rather, I started realizing that a lot of the poems I reshared and enjoyed were coming from the same account. After endless midnights spent in front of a computer screen, swallowing her work in bits and pieces, I ordered a copy of her first collection—*Honeybee*—which, at the time, was self-published. This was one of the first poetry collections I'd ever bought with my own money, and I eagerly awaited its arrival. So eagerly, in fact, that when it showed up on my doorstep I promptly read it from cover to cover, hardly taking a breath in between.

Despite never having gone through a breakup, despite the numerous distinctions between my life and Trista Mateer's, I felt seen and understood by her words. To read Mateer's early work is to remember what it is to be a teenage girl. You are messy with desire, thick with sentimentality. Everything feels like the end of the world because it is. Mateer writes, "It took me too long / to realize it was / not / romantic(, tender, or healthy) / to love someone else / more than I loved / myself," and I dog-eared the page, underlined each word with a shaky blue pen. This is what Mateer's work does to its readers—validates and comforts all in one fell swoop.

Since then, Mateer has amassed an audience both large in number and great in loyalty. In 2015, after self-publishing her second full-length collection *The Dogs I Have Kissed*, Mateer's audience rallied and voted for her to win the Goodreads Choice Award for Poetry. To have won this award with no agent, no publisher doing big-scale advertising, is a testament to the impact Mateer has on her readers. When she began traditionally publishing, it came to nobody's surprise—she has staying power, and *I Swear Somewhere This Works* proves it.

Foreword

  To be a poet on Tumblr in the early 2010s was unlike anything else that had happened before it, and unlike anything that's happened since. For a lot of writers, myself included, Tumblr's platform fostered a rich landscape of poetry, art, and prose, created by people that were just like them in age, time period, and sensibilities; this was a novelty. The collected and collaged work of artists growing up in the nineties and aughts weren't being taught in school or found obviously displayed on bookstore or library shelves. Creators on Tumblr were relatable, putting complex emotions into words and images that could instantly connect on a personal level with their audience. Logging onto your account and scrolling through your feed provided a wealth of quotes, poems, and inspiration. It was a melting pot of creativity.

  The poets that were writing and sharing on Tumblr during this time all displayed a certain flavor of raw honesty that felt daring, exciting, and fresh. This class of writers could post a poem lamenting heartbreak and, overnight, get thousands upon thousands of "notes," be reshared and liked across all corners of the internet. Given the nature of the website and its focus on "reblogging," you could then follow these writers and consume the art they enjoyed as well. Not only were these writers engaging, they were accessible. You could ask them questions and wait for them to post their answer, interact with them in comment sections of posts, read their sad poem and then laugh over a funny text post about their day. It was a community of young people excited to be sharing art, and their audience was growing by the day.

For anyone who
can't shut up
about love.

And for me.
  Let's not mince words.

Content Warning:
discussion of depression, death, and grief throughout
mentions of sexual assault on pages: 105, 108, 109, 110

Please note: portions of the text are from the author's social media, or were previously published.

This is a work of fiction. Names, characters, places, incidents etc. are either a product of the author's imagination or are used fictitiously and any resemblance to actual persons, living or dead, business establishments, events or locales is entirely coincidental.

Copyright © 2023 Trista Mateer. All rights reserved. No part of this book may be used or reproduced in any manner whatsoever without permission in writing from the author. This includes information storage and retrieval systems, data mining, and AI training. The only exception are in the case of clearly credited brief quotations for the purpose of articles, reviews, and marketing.

First edition.

Cover and Title Art by Arch Budzar
www.archbudzar.com

Interior Formatting & Images by Trista Mateer
Editing by Caitlin Conlon and Natalie Noland
Author photograph by Caitlyn Siehl

I SWEAR SOMEWHERE THIS WORKS

Paperback ISBN: 9798396319769   Hardcover ISBN: 798396665842

Printed in the United States of America.

For any inquiries please don't hesitate to get in touch.
tristamateerpoetry.com/contact

tristamateerpoetry.com

I SWEAR SOMEWHERE THIS WORKS

SELECTED POEMS
2013-2023

TRISTA MATEER

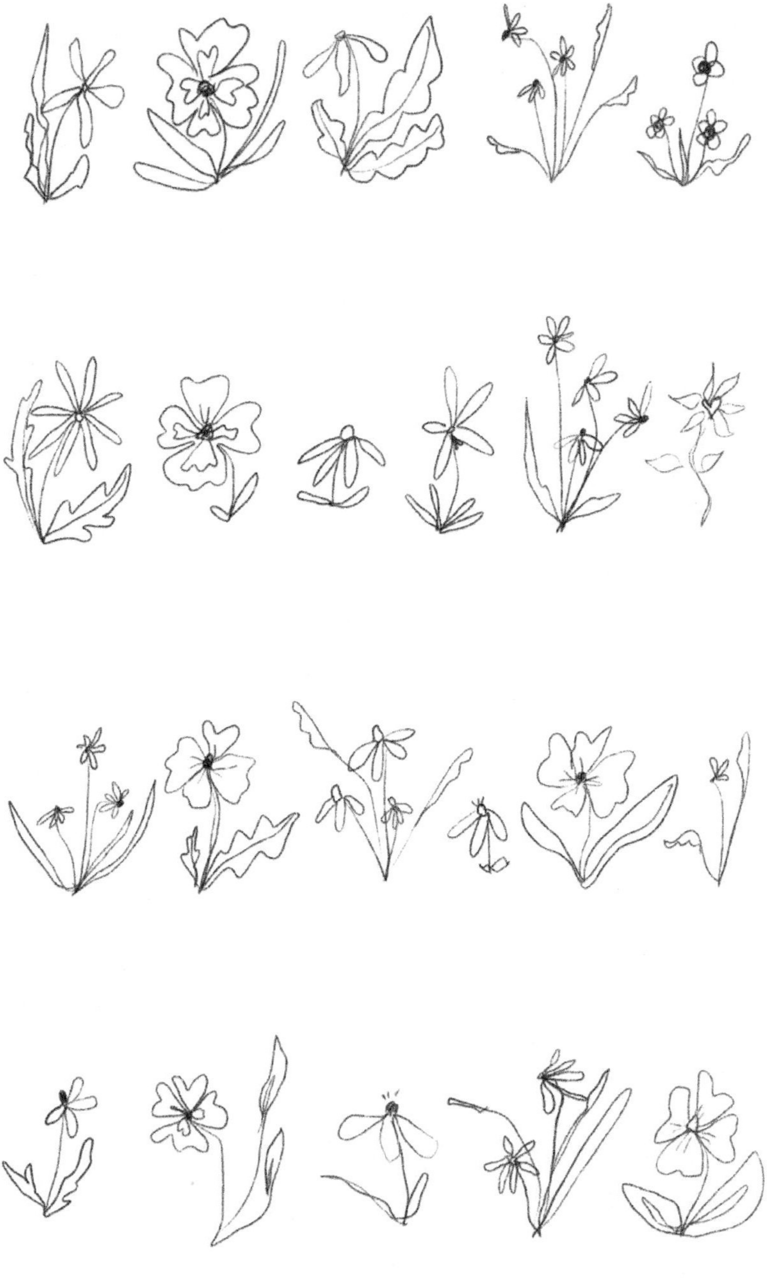

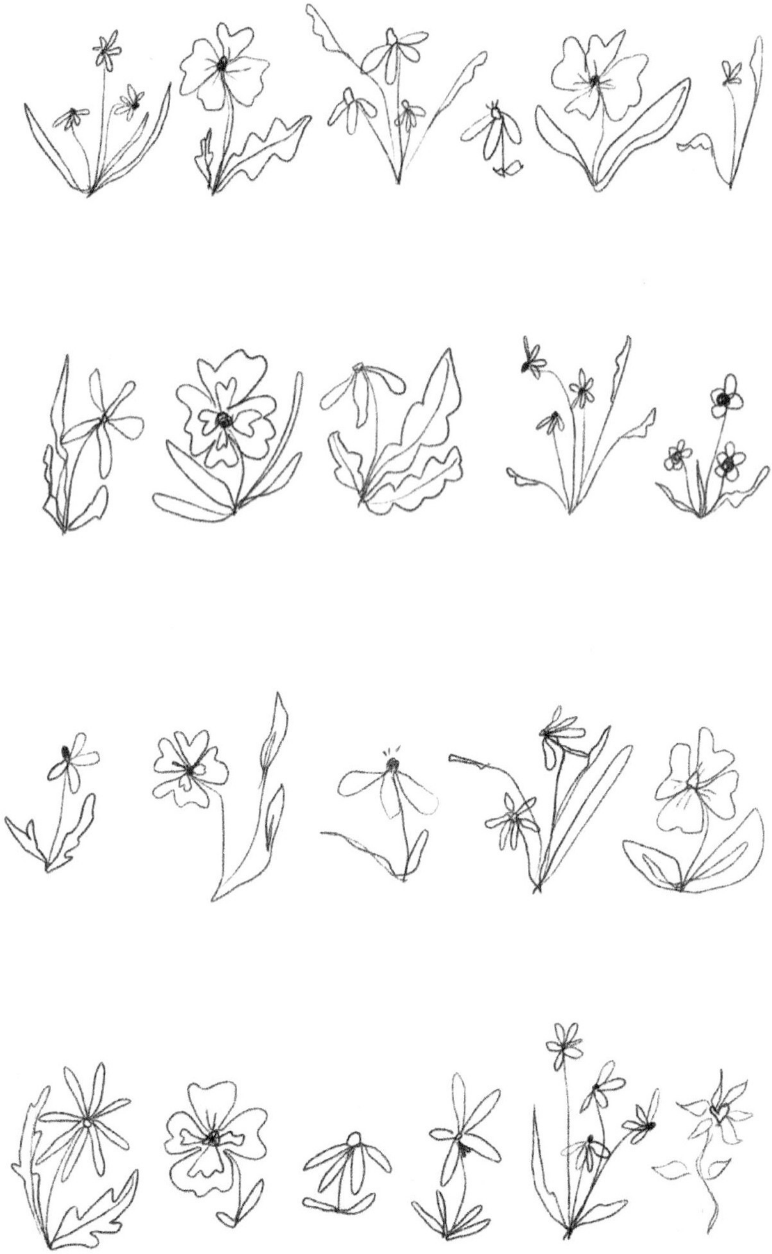

Other Books by Trista Mateer

The Myth & Magick series
    1. *Aphrodite Made Me Do It*
    2. *Artemis Made Me Do It*
    3. *Persephone Made Me Do It*

is it okay to say this? | collected brief excerpts + notes

girl, isolated | pandemic poems + mental health

When the Stars Wrote Back | young adult poetry

Honeybee | small town sapphic poetry

The Dogs I Have Kissed | weird dates & bad lovers

"Trista Mateer erupts with spells of thunder and then gifts you with a careful platter of language to cast them yourself."
(*Aphrodite Made Me Do It*)
— Blythe Baird, Author of *If My Body Could Speak*

"Trista has the rare talent of writing poems that are both good and true. In terms of literary art, this chapbook is brilliant."
(The Dogs I Have Kissed)
— Yena Sharma Purmasir, Author of *Viraha*

"How can something that hurts so much still be so tender? Mateer triumphs in this exploration. We are humbled to be witness."
(*Honeybee*)
— Ari Eastman, Author of *Bloodline*

"In *Honeybee*, Trista Mateer pulls the layers back on an old love and invites her readers to pick apart the pieces with her. She spares no one and nothing and the result is beautiful and awful and gorgeous and gut-wrenching."
— Fortesa Latifi, Author of *We Were Young*

"You will find grace between these pages and a little sadness, too—the kind that makes flowers grow in all of the places you need them most." (*Aphrodite Made Me Do It*)
— Wilder, Author of *Nocturnal*

"A beautiful tapestry of two interlocking narratives."
(*Before the First Kiss*)
— Rudy Francisco, Author of *No Gravity*

"A raw, painfully honest and beautiful documentation of the space between two people." *(Before the First Kiss)*
— Iain S. Thomas, Author of *I Wrote This for You*

"A moving time capsule of Mateer's most beautiful work."
(*I Swear Somewhere This Works*)
— Catarine Hancock, Author of *Shades of Lovers*

"Trista Mateer's works are an instruction guide for finding oneself. While Mateer explores a variety of themes from girlhood to love to grief, an open door connects them all. These poems will not only give you what you're looking for—they will also make space for you. In Mateer's poetry, there is no place you aren't welcome."
(*I Swear Somewhere This Works*)
— *Ari B. Cofer,* Author of *Paper Girl and the Knives that Made Her*

"Combined with the poet's own art, this book is a vibrant labyrinth, a treat for every reader. Mateer is magnificent as always."
(*Aphrodite Made Me Do It*)
— Nikita Gill, Author of *Wild Embers*

"*Artemis Made Me Do It* is a reminder that you can't keep femininity in a cage."
— Michaela Angemeer, Author of *You'll Come Back to Yourself*

"Trista Mateer has her pen on the pulse of girlhood."
(*Persephone Made Me Do It*)
— Caitlin Conlon, Author of *The Surrender Theory*

"Trista writes about love so honestly. It's messy, reckless hope. It's sticky-fingered stubbornness. This collection is a must-read for any queer femme, and for anyone who has ever lost themselves in a feverish want." *(Honeybee)*
— Clementine von Radics, Author of *Mouthful of Forevers*

"This is a collection that will beg you to be dogeared, coffee-stained, and shared." (*Honeybee*)
— Amanda Lovelace, Author of *the princess saves herself in this one*

Praise for Trista Mateer...

Winner - 2015 Goodreads Choice Awards — Poetry
(*The Dogs I Have Kissed*)

Finalist - 2019 Goodreads Choice Awards — Poetry
(*Aphrodite Made Me Do It*)

"Gut truths and gin-clear imagery, Trista Mateer reminds us of all those places left unexplored by language." (*Honeybee*)
— Foreword Reviews

"Mateer proves that young poets are creating communities of fans who love poetry on social media."
— CNN

"Trista Mateer is an absolute must-read for people with hearts that resemble gaping wounds."
— POPSUGAR

"[Mateer's] stream of consciousness autobiographical poems and short essays create the voyeuristic sense of reading someone's diary." (*When the Stars Wrote Back*)
— School Library Journal

"These poems are heartbreaking but still strangely hopeful."
(The Dogs I Have Kissed)
— BUZZFEED

"Simultaneously embodies tough wit and vulnerability."
(When the Stars Wrote Back)
— KIRKUS